Hermann Witte

Is the Euro Secure?

AF799022

Lingener Studien zu Management und Technik

herausgegeben von

Hermann Witte, Reinhard Rauscher
und Michael Ryba

Band 6

LIT

Hermann Witte

Is the Euro Secure?

Approach to a New Monetary Theory

LIT

This book is printed on acid-free paper.

Bibliografische Information der Deutschen Nationalbibliothek
Die Deutsche Nationalbibliothek verzeichnet diese Publikation in der Deutschen Nationalbibliografie; detaillierte bibliografische Daten sind im Internet über http://dnb.d-nb.de abrufbar.

ISBN 978-3-643-90833-9

A catalogue record for this book is available from the British Library

© LIT VERLAG GmbH & Co. KG Wien,
Zweigniederlassung Zürich 2016
Klosbachstr. 107
CH-8032 Zürich
Tel. +41 (0) 44-251 75 05
E-Mail: zuerich@lit-verlag.ch http://www.lit-verlag.ch

Distribution:

In the UK: Global Book Marketing, e-mail: mo@centralbooks.com
In North America: International Specialized Book Services, e-mail: orders@isbs.com
In Germany: LIT Verlag Fresnostr. 2, D-48159 Münster
Tel. +49 (0) 2 51-620 32 22, Fax +49 (0) 2 51-922 60 99, e-mail: vertrieb@lit-verlag.de
In Austria: Medienlogistik Pichler-ÖBZ, e-mail: mlo@medien-logistik.at
e-books are available at www.litwebshop.de

The euro can only be a stable currency in the macroeconomic equilibrium.

Only a stable, neutral, and a forgery-proof currency is a secure one.

Foreword

Germany has not only received a new currency with the introduction of the euro but has also gained new experiences unknown during the dm times.

At first the euro had been given the name “teuro”. Having encountered distress, supported by reports and estimates in the news media,[1] many citizens in European countries were asking whether their money had still been secure. It should be tried to give an answer to this specified issue in the following chapters.

First, it is important to describe basic monetary system structures to be able to understand these specific issues and meeting conditions, worked out in monetary literature, guaranteeing money security. Furthermore, possible alterations in monetary systems and methods of managing money are to be examined. Finally, it is necessary to examine whether there is a better theoretical basis for our monetary system than monetarism.[2]

Listed facts must be observed before the objectives of the European Union and especially the European Monetary Union are considered for discussion. These specific objectives enable judging successful introduction of the euros.

A summary from different possible considerations for conditions in which the euro is a secure currency is presented in detail.

There are basically three alternatives, evaluating the security of the euro: (1) Yes, the euro is secure, (2) No, the euro is not secure, and (3) it could be secure by achieving certain conditions. The third answer is the critical-constructive answer. Understood is that certain conditions must be achieved making the euro to a secure currency. This answer matches within the framework in the following line of thought.

I would like to thank Mr. Wendelin Heffner for translating the text.

Lingen, July 2016 Hermann Witte

---

[1] See i.e. Shambaugh, J.C./Reis, R./Rey, H.: The Euro´s Three Crises, in: Brookings Papers on Economic Activity, Spring 2012, pp. 157 – 231; Clairmont, F.F.: The Euro Crash, in: Economic and Political Weekly, Vol. 35 (2000), pp. 3644 - 3646

[2] See i.e. Friedman, M.: Die optimale Geldmenge und andere Essays, 2nd ed., München 1976 (1970[1])

Table of Contents

Illustration Register

Table Register

Abbreviation Register

ABl. EG/EU	Amtsblatt der EG/der EU (Official Bulletin of the European Community/Union)
BGBl.	Bundesgesetzblatt (Official Bulletin of the Republic of Germany)
CSR	Corporate Social Responsibility (gemeinsame soziale Verantwortung)
dm	"Deutsche Mark"
ECB	European Central Bank (Europäische Zentralbank, EZB)
ECOFIN-Rat	Rat der Wirtschafts- und Finanzminister der EU (Council of the Minsters of Economics and Finance of the EU)
Ed.	Editor (Herausgeber)
ed.	Edition (Auflage)
EFSF	Europäische Finanzstabilisierungsfazilität (European Financial Stabilization Facility)
EFSM	Europäischer Stabilisierungsmechanismus (European Financial Stabilization Mechanism)
EMU	European Monetary Union (Europäische Währungsunion, EWU)
ESCB	European System of Central Banks (Europäisches System der Zentralbanken, ESZB)
ESM	Europäischer Stabilitätsmechanismus (European Stabilization Mechanism)
EU	European Union
EuGH	Europäischer Gerichtshof (European Court of Law)
EWG	Europäische Wirtschaftsgemeinschaft (European Economic Community)
GDP	Gross Domestic Product
GmbH	Gesellschaft mit beschränkter Haftung (limited liability company)
GNP	Gross National Product
GWB	Gesetz gegen Wettbewerbsbeschränkungen (Act Against Limitation of Competition)

HdWW	Handwörterbuch der Wirtschaftswissenschaft (Handbook of Economic Sciences)
H.M.S.O.	Her Majesty´s Stationery Office
InsO	Insolvenzordnung (Insolvency Order)
IS	Zusammenhang von Sparen und Investitionen (connection between savings and investments)
LM	Zusammenhang von Liquidität und Geldmenge (connection between liquidity and amount of money)
MU	Money Unit (unit of a non-mentioned currency)
Repogeschäft	Reportgeschäft (carry-over business)
Slg.	Sammlung der Rechtsprechung des Gerichtshofes und des Gerichts Erster Instanz des EuGH (Collection of Jurisprudence of the Court of Justice and the Court of First Instance of the European Court of Justice)
SPV	Special Purpose Vehicle
StabWG	Gesetz zur Förderung der Stabilität und des Wachstums der Wirtschaft (Economic Stability and Growth Law)
UWG	Gesetz gegen den unlauteren Wettbewerb (Law Against Unfair Competition)

Introduction: Assignments, activities, and objectives of the European Union and the European Monetary Union

Responsibilities of the European Community (EC) have been determined in Art. 2 of the Contract of the Founding of the European Community. These responsibilities are also valid for the European Union and determined. Thus setting up of regulations of a Common Market and of an Economic- and Monetary Union.[3]

Responsibilities of the European Community and thus the European Union are established in Art. 3 in the Contract of the Founding of the European Community.[4] Responsibilities of the Community - respectively of the Union, economy -, and monetary union have been established in Art. 3a of the contract. Sentence (2) is of interest in the framework described in this book. This particular sentence states that: "die unwiderrufliche Festlegung der Wechselkurse im Hinblick auf die Einführung einer einheitlichen Währung, ..., sowie die Festlegung und Durchführung einer einheitlichen Geld- sowie Wechselkurspolitik ... (the irrevocable determination of the exchange rates, regarding introduction of a uniform currency, ... as well as determining and implementing a uniform money- as well as exchange rate policy ...)."[5]

Determined formulated responsibilities and activities from the European Community – also completed for the European Union – have been contractually established by the European Union (Maastricht-Contract). The Article A of the contract reads: "Grundlage der Union sind die Europäischen Gemeinschaften, ergänzt durch die in diesem Vertrag eingeführten Politiken und Formen der Zusammenarbeit (Basics of the Union are the European Communities, supplemented by this particular introduced policies and forms of collaborations)."[6]

Objectives of the European Union have been established in Article B of the Contract – introducing an economic- and monetary union as well as a uniform currency.[7]

Details for introducing an economic- and monetary union have been determined in Part VI, the economy- and monetary union, of the Contract of the European Community[8] as well as the 3rd Protocol to the Contract of the European Union.[9]

---

[3] See Art. 2 Vertrag zur Gründung der Europäischen Gemeinschaft vom 25. März 1957 BGBL. II p. 766, in der Fassung des Vertrages über die Europäische Union vom 7. Februar 1992, ABL. EG Nr. C 224 vom 31. August 1992, p. 6

[4] See Art. 3 Vertrag zur Gründung der Europäischen Gemeinschaft ...

[5] Art. 3a. (2) Vertrag zur Gründung der Europäischen Gemeinschaft ...

[6] Artikel A Vertrag über die Europäische Union (Maastricht-Vertrag) vom 7. Februar 1992, ABL. EG Nr. C 224 vom 31. August 1992

[7] See Artikel B Vertrag über die Europäische Union ...

[8] See Teil VI. Vertrag zur Gründung der Europäischen Gemeinschaft ...

The objective of the Monetary Union is formulated through the objective of European Central Bank (ECB) in Art. 105 of the Contract of the Founding of the European Community[10] and Art. 2 of the protocol to the Contract of the European Union.[11] Priority objective of the ECB is the guarantee of the price stability in supporting general economic policies in the community respectively union.[12]

Principally, connected ideas with introducing a European Economy- and Monetary Union is not new. The Swedish economist Knut Wicksell already wrote in the year 1898:

"... eine rationelle Geldreform ... (gehört) ... zu den wichtigsten ... volkswirtschaftlichen Fragen ... (sie bedarf der) Durchführung notwendiger internationaler Vereinbarungen von dauernder ... Art .... In jedem Schritt zur Zusammenschließung der Völker für wirtschaftliche oder wissenschaftliche Zwecke ... (liegt) ... eine neue Garantie für die Wahrung ... desjenigen Gutes, von dem das ... Erreichen aller anderen ... Güter ... abhängt – des internationalen Friedens (... a rational monetary reform ... (belongs) ... to the most important ... macroeconomic issues ...(it is necessary) implementation of necessary international agreements of long lasting ... kind...In every step merging nations for economic- or scientific purposes ... (lies) .... a new guarantee for maintaining ... of the particular good, of the ... achieving of all other ... goods ... depending - on the international peace)."[13]

---

[9] See Vertrag über die Europäische Union ..., 3. Protokoll über die Satzung des Europäischen Systems der Zentralbanken und der Europäischen Zentralbank

[10] See Vertrag zur Gründung der Europäischen Gemeinschaft, Art. 105

[11] See Vertrag über die Europäische Union ..., 3. Protokoll über die Satzung des Europäischen Systems der Zentralbanken und der Europäischen Zentralbank, Art. 2

[12] To critics regarding the European Monetary Union and euro see i.e. Duwendag, D.: Akzeptanzprobleme der Europäischen Währungsunion, in: Review of Economics, Vol. 47 (1996), pp. 241 – 263; Issing, O.: Von der D-Mark zum Euro, Tübingen 1998, esp. pp. 30 - 32

[13] Wicksell, K.: Geldzins und Güterpreis, München 2006 (Org. Jena 1898), p. 232

Part 1: Basic Structures of Monetary Systems in Market Economies

Basic structures of market economies with a monetary system can be easily presented by means of the following illustration.

Fig. 1: The basic structure of a given market economy with one monetary system

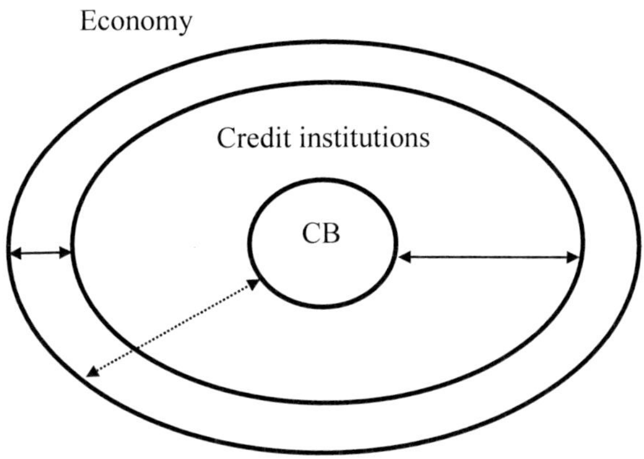

Source: own presentation

The Central Bank (CB) is located in the center of the system because it circulates the bank notes – for that particular reason, it is also called the issue bank. Credit institutions are established in the middle of the oval field. The external oval field represents the actual economy. This particular area emphasizes market activities (suppliers, buyers, companies, private households and public authorities, associations etc.) They are excluded from central banks as well as credit institutions. They are referred to as "non-credit economic units". Important components of markets, except "non-credit economic units" are located in external oval areas. Total markets are divided up into three main-component markets, goods-, labor-, and monetary markets. Three main-component markets again are subdivided into a multitude of partial goods-, partial labor-, and partial-monetary markets. There is a small component of these markets in the internal and middle oval areas.

Limiting and therefore identifying economic units and markets has not been achieved yet. Central banks and credit institutions are also economic units. These economic units are on goods- and labor-markets active, too. But not all of these economic units are located in external ovals. The monetary market is reverse. Most of it is located in internal- and central oval areas. Central banks are responsible for processing economic monetary unit activities - especially with central bank money - between internally located oval areas – the central banks – and centrally located oval areas – the credit institutions. Consequently, these specified partial-monetary markets are referred to as central bank markets.

Economic units are primarily responsible for product manufacture (material goods and services) needed by the economy and additionally for employment provision, so that economic units are enabled to purchase manufactured products. Economic manufacturing units have to offer products on goods markets. Employable economy units (citizens) in return should then offer their manpower on labor markets. Just as credit institutions demonstrate a connection between internal and external connection, monetary markets should assure goods- and labor markets. Changing monetary markets into individual entities can have clear negative results on economic circulations.

1. Central Bank

Central banks are institutions, autonomous of states respectively governments. Central banks are authorized to meet decisions without any instructions issued by governments. Central banks are responsible to support policies of governments with their decisions/measures.

Major responsibility for central banks is to issue bank notes, referred to as currency components and a further duty defined - stability safeguarding (money stability) the value of currencies.

Central banks are responsible for circulating money supplies on markets necessary for all exchange activities carried out on markets. If there is not enough money in circulation, exchange activities could be slowed down. Economy would be aggravated. If there is too much money in circulation, the opposite will take place. Even though all exchange activities can be performed – monetary- and goods markets are unbalanced. Superfluous money can then lead to inefficient behavior in economic units. Circumstantially, this can also cause inflation.

Four possible instruments for protecting currency stability[14] are available. These include (1) minimum reserve policy, (2) refinancing policy, (3) open market policy, and (4) foreign exchange policy. The first three instruments are related directly to the currency, protected by central banks. The fourth instrument controls relationships to foreign currencies and protects its own currency against external influences.

Minimum reserve policies pursue minimum reserve rate changes. Minimum reserves are assets of credit institutions maintained at central banks because of statutory minimum reserve obligations for demand-, savings-, and time deposits,

[14] See the instruments of monetary policy and the central bank i.e. Spahn, H.-P.: Geldpolitik, 2nd ed., München 2009, pp. 89 - 115

as well as raised money with a maturity of up to four years. Minimum reserve rates determine percentages of mentioned deposits, credit institutions have to deposit - as assets interest-free - at central banks. Central banks influence with this specified instrument directly money – and credit creation scopes of credit institutions and indirectly economic units in external oval areas. If central banks change minimum reserve conditions, then credit institutions themselves will change credit- and deposit conditions for economic units. Thus, scopes of economic units and ultimately circles of economic processes will be influenced. Central banks provide credit institutions with central bank money. An increase of minimum reserve rates cause reductions of mentioned scopes and liquidity in economic cycles. Respectively, a decrease of minimum reserves lead to increases of the mentioned scopes and liquidity. Additionally, a second effect results from changes of minimum reserve rates. Interest rates change. Since credit institutes have to maintain increases of higher minimum reserve rates (money) – interest-free - interest rates increase. However, if minimum reserve rates decrease, interest-free capital will decrease for credit institutions at central banks and interest rates decrease on monetary markets.

Central banks deal with condition changes in their refinancing policies enabling credit institutions to refinance themselves. The term refinancing describes processes of credit financing distributed by other credit institutions – central banks. Central banks can influence directly the credit behavior of credit institutions by changing amounts or respectively levels of credit volumes (allotments) and credit interest rates. Additionally, central banks determine specific (high) requirements toward quality and prerequisites, regarding security conditions and (discountable) bills of exchange. By means of refinancing policies, credit behavior of economic units are controlled indirectly in external oval areas. Consequently, quota increase cause higher volumes of credit institution loans at central banks. Central bank money supplies are increased. Credit institutions themselves deal with more credits and increase money supplies. Quota decreases cause reverse effects. Accordingly, interest rate increases at central banks lead to credits decreases which are dealt with by credit institutions. However, interest rate decreases cause the opposite. Refinancing policies are subdivided into two sectors: (1) Lombard- and (2) discount policy.

The Lombard policy considers refinancing credit institutions at central banks by means of pledging commodities and securities. Central banks publish a Lombard directory, listing fixed-income securities it has accepted. In addition, central banks determine a Lombard line and a Lombard rate. The Lombard line determines upper limits central banks deal with the Lombard credits. The Lombard rate is the interest rate credit institutions have to pay.

In the framework of discount policies central banks buy exchange-bills against deductions of interests (discounts) from credit institutions (accepted). Thus, regularly, central banks do not raise commissions. Central banks determine levels respectively volumes of discount credits (discount contingent rates). Key interest rates determined by central banks – the Lombard- and discount rates are referred to as base rates. Credit institutions orient themselves on these specified interest rates.

Open market policies are additional instruments of central banks. Thus, central banks are enabled to directly influence central bank supplies respectively credit behavior of credit institutions and non-credit institutions and indirectly, credit behavior on economy units in external oval areas by selling and purchasing fixed-interest securities and money market instruments on central bank money respectively on their own account respectively at credit institutions and non-credit institutions. Markets for these transactions are referred to as open markets because not only central banks and non-credit institutions are market active. There is a distinction between quantities and fixed rates. Central banks sell or buy certain above mentioned security quantities. Purchasing, causes increases in central bank money stocks – whereas selling – consequently, leads to a reduction of central bank stocks. Fixed rates describe the length of time sales or purchases taking place by central banks - until a certain security has been reached on markets.

Central bank exchange policy is limiting growing influences on domestic monetary policies. Foreign currency payments in form of assets, checks, and exchange bills paid in foreign currencies in foreign countries are called existing claims. Central bank foreign exchange policies are divided into (1) swap policy and (2) policy of similar activities on foreign exchange markets such as pension- and outright time activities. In the framework of the swap policy, central banks buy and sell - per cash simultaneously per time - foreign exchanges. Central banks provide credit institutions with central bank money supplies with these specific measures. However, should central banks sell and purchase foreign exchange simultaneously, per fixed date, central bank money will be reduced. Resulting differences between sale- and purchasing rates on free exchange markets are defined as swap rates. Central banks determine additional manipulated swap rates to exchange market formed swap rates. Central banks utilize these swap rates to cause credit institutions selling or purchasing foreign exchanges.

Summarizing, central banks are able to apply different instruments to control and protect the economy. Central banks are responsible for guaranteeing currency stability of countries, protecting of economy against inflation, deflation, and external economic influences. Presentation of instruments and of their effectiveness emphasizes that central bank stocks (money basis), money supplies, interest rates, liquidity play important roles for this protection. These parameters are also referred to as intermediate objectives because first they have to achieve objective specters to finally reach objectives for economy controls into desired directions.

2. Credit Institutions

Credit institutions located in middle oval areas (see fig. 1) are connected between inner ovals, central banks, and market actives (suppliers, buyers, companies, private and official households, associations, etc.) in external oval areas. Credit institutions are responsible to provide market participants with money located in external oval areas, and to implement policies of central banks in controlling the economy. This is achieved by deposit- and credit activities. Furthermore, they have been concerned with additional activities (such as procurement of insurances, travel arrangements, etc.).

They have been subdivided roughly into four groups in the Federal Republic of Germany: (1) commercial banks, (2) savings banks, (3) cooperative- and agricultural banks, and (4) special credit institutions. Distinctions between the four groups' origin and consequently also judicial regulations and activities have been considerably, clearly noted. Nevertheless, all four groups adhere to the original activities of credit institutions.

3. "Noncredit Economic" Economy Units

The actual economy takes place in external oval areas. Considering market actives (such as: suppliers, buyers, companies, private- and public budgets, associations, etc.), not counting to central banks nor to credit institutions; they have been originally described as "non-credit economic units". Next to "non-credit economic units", essential market components are located in external areas. Total markets are divided up into three main partial markets: goods-, labor-, and monetary markets. Smaller parts of markets are located in internal- and middle oval areas.

Economic units are responsible for a) manufacturing goods (material goods and services) needed by the economy, and b) in providing employment, so that economic units are enabled to earn money buying products. Thus, manufacturing economic units (companies) have to offer products on goods markets – whereas working economic units (citizens) have to offer their manpower on labor markets. Just as credit institutions in middle oval areas create connections between internal and external oval areas, monetary markets assure connections between product- and labor markets. However, by reaching independence, monetary markets are causing considerable impacts on economy cycles.

4. Government

The essential factor influencing the economy and monetary systems in fig. 1 is missing. It is the government of a nation. Since governments are not present in the graph, it is assumed, that they do not have any respectively have just a little direct influence on monetary systems and do not have attributed controls over the economy. Governments have just one direct influence – providing (of coinage rights) coins. It is understood that coins are metal-pieces used for money. They are cash and thus counted to money supplies. Governments consequently, have some influence controlling money supplies that have been adjusted to proportions of coins to money controls taken into consideration - money amount M_3 (compare 6.2). A direct and strong government influence on interest rates and liquidity is not possible. Government influence on monetary systems and the economy is to be described as indirect. Government can practice indirect influence on structures and processes of monetary systems as well as the economy through legislation (preparation as well as submission of laws) and supervision (i.e. control and supervision of banks) (cf. Fig. 2).

Fig. 2: Influence of governments and lobbyists on an economy with a monetary system

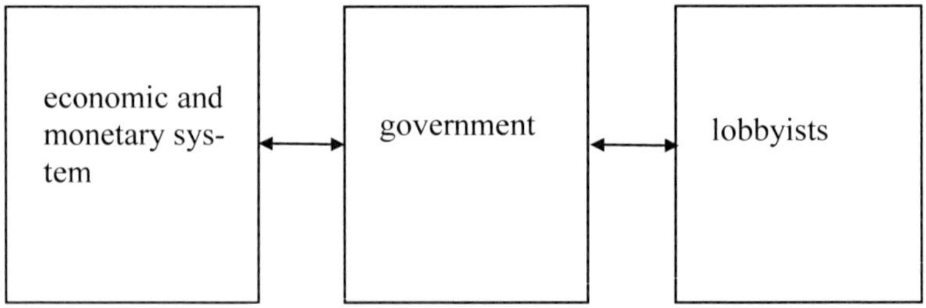

Source: own presentations

5. Lobbyists

Lobbyists are stakeholders making contacts with representatives and (original the colonnade/lobby in the parliament building) contact to government officials influencing governments in preparations of laws, etc. and influencing votes in parliaments - according to their own interests. This particular method demonstrates an indirect influence, created on structures and processes on monetary- and economy systems (cf. fig. 2). Power of this indirect influence is difficult to estimate. It depends on two components: (1) intensity of lobby and (2) influence of parliamentarians and government members. However, it is clear, lobbying is a tradition, in the sense "of the will of the "People" carried democracies.

6. Control of the Economy by Means of Monetary Policies

Presenting instruments of central banks have shown that controlling the economy by central banks consists of principally four parameters. These parameters are: (1) central bank money amount (money basis), (2) money amount, (3) interest rates, and (4) liquidity. Since central banks and money supplies depend on each other, theories controlling the economy principally are to be reduced to three same sized theory blocks. Thus, strategies to control the economy can be derived from these particular theories. It is now important to discuss theories and strategies.

6.1 Interest Control According to Keynes

Monetary market control by varying interest rates goes back to Keynes and Keynesians. Keynes's approach is based on the assumption that economy units spend the achieved income – is primarily intended to be used for consumption interests. Taking also into account durable goods, listed as consumer goods. The other part of income is saved by economic units in one form or another. Furthermore, Keynes has anticipated that in a national economy amounts of savings equalize amount of investments. Again investments signify increase in endowments of capital respectively improvement of performances of national economies. In regarding interest rates, Keynes[15] concluded, that "Änderungen im Zinssatz auf den tatsächlich ersparten Betrag ... von allerhöchster Bedeutung (sind) (changes in interest rates on actual saved amounts ... (are) of an utmost significance)".[16] Saving and investing are according to Keynes, dependent on the interest rate.

However, Keynes has not only recognized the importance for controlling a national economy but also the significance of money supplies and liquidity. He equalizes money supplies to interest rates, depending on liquidity preference.[17] Keynes divides money supplies into two components: (1) partial money amount 1, maintaining economy units consisting of transaction- and precautionary motives, and (2) partial money amount 2. Keynes appropriately works with two liquidity functions: (1) liquidity function 1, they - above all – depend on the income level and (2) liquidity function 2, depending essentially on ratio of current interest rates and to existing expectations.[18]

Since central banks do not have direct influence on income levels and expectations - the interest controlled approach by Keynes results in the interest rate control. Central banks are able to control key interest rates (Lombard- and discount rate) and thus control the economy.

However, as it is known today - interest control does not function properly. Interest-controlled monetary policy has been rocked by the "lag-doctrine" set up by Friedman. Friedman has found time lags in empirical studies. Changes of

[15] See Keynes, J.M.: Allgemeine Theorie der Beschäftigung, des Zinses und des Geldes, 11th ed., Berlin 2009, i.e. pp. 46, 55, 65, 77 ff., 140 ff.

[16] Keynes, J.M.: Allgemeine Theorie ..., p. 94

[17] See Keynes, J.M.: Allgemeine Theorie ..., p. 142

[18] See Keynes, J.M.: Allgemeine Theorie ..., p. 168

monetary policies have become effective, partly after considerable delays.[19] These effects have been compared with today's handling with water pipes, turning on faucets - and water flowing after months (6, 9, 12, or 16).[20] Even though, some opponents, unconvinced with the empirical basics of the “lag-doctrine” (i.e. Culbertson), (it is known that) Friedman has enforced his studies. This has led to revival of the quantity theory and to a change in monetary policy. Monetary policy based on Keynes's ideas has been superseded by the neo-quantity-oriented monetary policy. Friedman's ideas on the monetary theory and monetary policy are dominating today's policy.

6.2 Monetary Control by Quantity Theoreticians and Monetarists

Monetary control dates back to the quantity theory. Keynes has demonstrated weaknesses of this theory and thus, has led to a revolution on monetary policies. Money amount control has then been set up on a new basis (the neo-quantity theory), based on criticisms made by Friedman on Keynes's quantity theory. The counter revolution has then led – as it is generally known - to a new change in monetary policy.

Based on the quantity theory, the thesis is: the economy is better off, respectively quicker, controlled by changes of money supplies, than by variations of interest rates. Time lags in interest rate changes can be directed to influence undesired economy processes. Economic situations can have changed during time lags in such a way, that opposite (undesired) effects have taken place.

Change of money supplies have been caused by results - according to the quantity theory by the Fisher's Exchange Equation.[21] The equation creates an equilibrium of money- and economic processes of goods of a national economy – in other words - money supplies and money demands. Money supplies multiplied by velocities of money (also named an income cycle velocity) and equalized to exchange- respectively trading volumes, multiplied by price levels. Money amount M_3 is used for economic controls. The calculation of money amount M_3 is performed by adding money amount M_1 and M_2. Money amount components (aggregates) are to be taken from table 1.

---

[19] See Friedman, M.: A Program for Monetary Stability, in: Ketchum, M.D./Kendall, L.T. (Ed.): Readings in Financial Institutions, Boston 1965, pp. 189 - 209; Friedman, M.: The Lag in Effect of Monetary Policy, in: Journal Political Economy, Vol. 69 (1961), pp. 447 - 466

[20] See Culbertson, J.M.: Friedman on the Lag in Effect of Monetary Policy, in: Journal of Political Economy, Vol. 78 (1960), S. 617 – 621, here pp. 617 f.

[21] See Fisher, I.: The Purchasing Power of Money, New York 1911, pp. 24 – 28, 47 – 49, 53 – 54, 149 - 183

Tab. 1: Structure of the components of the money amount

	components of the money amounts M_1, M_2 and M_3
M_1 =	cash (without cash balances of Banks) + sight deposits (daily maturing capital contributions) domestic non-Banks at credit institutions
M_2 =	M_1 + term deposits up to 2 years inland non-Banks at the credit institutions + deposits with an agreed upon notice period of up to 3 months
M_3 =	M_1, M_2 + repo transactions + shares in money business market fund shares as well as bonds up to 2 years

Source: own presentation according to the European Central Bank: Money report 1999, Frankfurt 1999, p. 35

The velocity of money is assumed to be short-termed so that the price level of money amount can be calculated with the knowledge of the exchange volume, provided by the central bank for the purpose of circulating it. The exchange volume can be determined by means of the gross national product[22] or a similar parameter (gross domestic product, national income). The price-level is a percentage value related to a basis year (= 100) and indicates adjustments opposite the basis year. Based on possible different parameters using the exchange volume, there are different variants of the Fisher Equation of Exchange available.[23]

Keynes has exercised serious criticism on the economy and thus also on the quantity theory. He has criticized the contradiction in the explanation of prices.[24] Usually, prices are explained with supply- and demand curves. In this context, prices only depend on amount of supply or demand respectively appropriate elasticities. This simplified, generally accepted appropriate assumption has often been neglected and above all, it has been neglected in the monetary theory. Money mostly depends on the velocity of money (income circulation velocity), hoarding, saving as well as inflation and deflation. Usually, there is no creation of relationships to elasticity taking place. Keynes has concluded, that "die Elastizität des Angebots gleich Null und die Nachfrage proportional der Geldmenge geworden sein muß … (elasticity of offers equalize to zero and demands, have to be proportional to money supplies ...)".[25] Thus, discussions just vaporize – nothing becomes clear and everything is possible.[26] Keynes has not directly referred to the quantity theory.

From the presented dependent relationships it becomes very clear that the criticisms on the quantity equation respectively the Fisher Equation of Exchange refers to the quantity theory. Criticism issues on the quantity theory brought for-

[22] The German Board of Statistics is working with the term "Bruttonationaleinkommen".
[23] See for a survey Woll, A.: Quantitätstheorie, in: Handwörterbuch der Wirtschaftswissenschaft (HdWW), 6. Vol., Stuttgart a.o. 1981, pp. 392 – 399
[24] See Keynes, J.M.: Allgemeine Theorie …, p. 247
[25] Keynes, J.M.: Allgemeine Theorie …, p. 247
[26] See Keynes, J.M.: Allgemeine Theorie …, p. 247

ward by Keynes have been mostly reduced to the following three arguments in literature. Criticized is that (1) the basic quantity equation (a variant of the Fisher Exchange Equation) has just been a (always fulfilled) tautology, (2) full employment has been assumed, and (3) velocity of money is instable.[27]

Based on criticisms by Keynes, Friedman[28] above all, has carried out improvements on the quantity theory, so that discussion topics have been on neo-quantity theory and monetarism. He has adjusted the quantity theory to a demand for money instead of the theory of prices or outputs. Additionally, he has introduced a stable relationship between the demand for a real cash management and a limited number of parameters.[29]

However, Friedman has not only caused adjustments on the quantity theory but he has also demonstrated in tests with long number series, that the quantity theory or rather the neo-quantity theory for the United States of America has led to a better control of the economy than the "Keynesian Economy".[30]

The neo-quantity theory assumes an empiric tested stable demand function for money demonstrating effects of the theory and discusses arguments against the "Keynesian Economy".[31]

Later Friedman has met a long known criticism on the quantity theory – at the beginning, it has not been weakened by the neo-quantity theory. This is the thesis of the "banking school", that the quantity theory has been inappropriate "weil das Geldangebot passiv auf die Geldnachfrage reagier(t)e; … (because money supplies have been passive towards money reacted demands (reacts))."[32] This particular criticism has been suspended by Friedman and Schwartz with a study on money history.[33] Topic in this study was that money amounts can be deter-

---

[27] See Johnson, H.: Neue Entwicklungen in der Geldtheorie: Ein Kommentar, in: Brunner, K./Monissen, H.G./Neumann, M.J.M (Ed.): Geldtheorie, Köln 1974, pp. 26 – 48, here p. 27

[28] See Friedman, M.: The Quantity Theory of Money - A Restatement, in: Friedman, M. (Ed.): Studies in the Quantity Theory of Money, Chicago 1956, pp. 3 - 21; see also Friedman, M.: The Optimum Quantity of Money and Other Essays, London a.o. 1969, pp. 51 – 79 (German: Friedman, M.: Die optimale Geldmenge und andere Essays, 2nd ed., München 1976 (1970[1]), esp. pp. 77 - 99)

[29] See Friedman, M.: The Quantity Theory ..., pp. 56 - 59 (German: Friedman, M.: Die optimale Geldmenge …, pp. 84 – 87); see also Johnson, H.: Neue Entwicklungen in der Geldtheorie ..., p. 27

[30] See Friedman, M./Meiselman, D.: The relative Stability of Monetary Velocity and the Investment Multiplier in the United States , 1897 – 1958, in: Commission on Money and Credit: Stabilization Policies, Englewoods Cliffs, N.J. 1963, pp. 165 – 268, esp. pp. 165 f.

[31] See Johnson, H.: Neue Entwicklungen in der Geldtheorie …, p. 27

[32] See Johnson, H.: Neue Entwicklungen in der Geldtheorie …, p. 27

[33] See Friedman, M./Schwartz, A.: A Monetary History of the United States, 1867 – 1960, Princeton, N.J. 1963, pp. 676 -700, esp. p. 676

mined independently and that money amount variations have statistically significant effects on economic developments.[34]

6.3 Liquidity Control of Liquidity Theoreticians

The third block of the monetary theory and -policy is the liquidity theory of money. Liquidity theoreticians have been emphasizing the thesis that money amounts have not provided sufficient basis for controlling the economy. They have rather supposed a control, based on liquidity because liquidity of an economic unit is responsible for dealing with expenditures of economic units. First of all, the term liquidity has to be explained. Liquidity of individual economic units is to be calculated to the overall liquidity in the economic environment. Thus, this factor can achieve control of a national economy. Liquidity theory has in principle two basic approaches. First, "Economy by Keynes" and then it is presented in detail in the "Radcliffe Report"[35] - a concept of liquidity control. Keynes has assumed that money supplies consist of two components: A predominant dependent liquidity function 1 and above all, from the relationship of the current interest rate and of existing expectations depending on liquidity functions.[36] The term "liquidity" respectively "liquidity preference" has not just been determined monetarily, but also non-monetarily. Non-monetary assets and liabilities are added to liquidity.[37] Broad interpretations of the term liquidity also clarify that liquidity itself represents a narrow interpretation, far more than just as money - respectively money quantity. Thus, from the money quantity considerable deviant concept and considerable comprehensive indicator is revealed by controlling a national economy. Free liquidity reserves as indicators respectively intermediate objectives for certain periods in the spectra of central banks.

This extension of the term liquidity leads ultimately to the conclusion that all goods, in a specified economic unit as well as liability, should be seen as liquidity. Free goods or goods that are based on missing demands cannot obtain a price respectively cannot specify a price. In calculating the liquidity, amortizations and value losses must be considered.

---

[34] See a short presentation of the results of the study done by Friedman and Schwartz; see also Johnson, H.: Neue Entwicklungen in der Geldtheorie ..., p. 28

[35] See Committee on the Working of the Monetary System: REPORT, London 1959 (H.M.S.O.; Cmnd. 827), esp. pp. 107, 337; see also Kaldor, N.: The Radcliffe Report, in: The Review of Economics and Statistics, Vol. 42 (1960), pp. 14 – 19; Gurlery, J. G.: The Radcliffe Report and Evidence, in: The American Economic Review, Vol. 50 (1960), pp. 672 – 700; Jucker-Fleetwood, E.E.: Der Radcliffe Report, in: Zeitschrift für die gesamte Staatswissenschaft, Vol. 116 (1960), pp. 500 – 517, here p. 512

[36] See Keynes, J.M.: Allgemeine Theorie ..., p. 168

[37] See Paish, F.W.: Was ist Liquidität eigentlich? In: Dürr, E. (Ed.): Geld- und Bankpolitik, 2nd ed., Köln 1971, pp. 283 – 291, here p. 285; see also Rose, H.B.: Monetary Policy and the Capital Market, 1955-56, in: The Economic Journal, Vol. 67 (1957), pp. 397 – 414, here pp. 398 ff.; Gaskin, M.: Liquidity and Monetary Mechanism, in: Oxford Economic Papers, Vol. 12 (1960), S. 274 – 293, here p. 275

6.4 Mixture of Three Control Mechanisms in Practical Monetary Policies

Display of the three blocks of monetary theory and monetary policy demonstrates discussions on mixtures of two, and - earlier of three theories. "Policy-mix", is respectively has been achieved. "Policy-mix" has also been recognized as an instrument of central banks. Minimum reserve policy affects money supplies, liquidity, and interest rates. Refinancing policy has impacts on interest rates and determinations of contingents – also on money supplies and liquidity. Money supplies, liquidity, and interest rates are also influenced by open market policies. Foreign exchange policy causes the same impacts on liquidity and interest rates.

It is questionable whether improved controls of national economies lead to, or whether detrimental effects approach each other, thereby achieving the three theories. The question will be taken up in the following chapter.

6.5 Consequences arising from a Mixture of Three different aligned Approaches

Evaluation criteria respectively benchmarks are necessary to evaluate the three approaches to control a national economy. This evaluation criteria has been in the economic tradition; the ability to create an economic equilibrium (marketing equilibrium). The achievement of the economic equilibrium has probably been seen as the major objective of the economy ever since Adam Smith[38] has developed it. Assumed is, that this objective is much older. Achievement of equilibria has also been seen as a priority objective in other scientific disciplines (such as: physics, medicine, etc.). One can easily understand this objective. Disequilibrium is defined as a crisis in economy, disease in medicine, and instability in physics. Those consequences are definitely undesired and have to be avoided.

It is not really easy to evaluate the approach of achieving equilibria as objectives suggested by Keynes. This difficulty is caused by the fact, that the presentation of the developed approach by Keynes has to be roughly divided into two sectors. First, one can refer to the "Economy of Keynes" and second, to the "Keynesian Economy". Since both approaches are not identical, a clear distinction needs to be drawn. The IS-ML-Graph reduced approach to the "Keynesian Economy" developed by Keynes's successors, has been classified as less subtle and thor-

[38] See the appreciation of the work, in: Smith, A.: Der Wohlstand der Nationen, 12th ed., München 2009, pp. XV – LXXIX, here p. LVI

ough by Leijonhufvud than the original approach by Keynes, "Economy from Keynes".[39]

"Keynesian Economy" lays out the approach from Keynes through the IS-LM-Graph as an underemployment equilibrium.[40] Leijonhufvud shows the approach in his interpretation from Keynes, that Keynes has been against an adjustment process leading directly to a market equilibrium by price changes. Leijonhufvud has turned against the prevailing doctrine and has developed a dynamic process on quantity adjustments based on destabilizing retroactive effects.[41] In short, Leijonhufvud has argued that the approach of Keynes to underemployment equilibria has other causes.

Regardless of interpretation differences, it was noted that the equilibrium emphasized by Keynes is a partial and a very special one. On one hand, Keynes considers it as just a quantitative equilibrium, classified as a partial equilibrium. It is not a total equilibrium because value-based considerations have been neglected. Otherwise one has to question critically whether an equilibrium can be seen as an economical equilibrium in situations of underemployment. There is a disequilibrium on the labor market that cannot stay logically on the goods- and money market without any retroactive effects. These results have been based on hierarchy- and non-compensation principles. Equilibria are in a hierarchy, and a disequilibrium cannot be transferred into an equilibrium. However, if there is an equilibrium in the approach of Keynes, mentioned on both markets, then it can only be the result of special assumptions and/or of inappropriate interpretations of equilibria. Requesting a total (quantity- and value-based) equilibrium, an equilibrium at an underemployment situation, as demonstrated by Keynes, would be impossible respectively not at an equilibrium stage.

Findings of Keynes have been based on basic assumptions of disequilibria situations. Economic units have already been located in assumed initial situations in disequilibria situations - according to Keynes. One should begin with the smallest economic units of national economies - that is - start to request quantity- as well as value-based equilibria. If revenues (incomes) are equal to costs (expenditures) then the economic units will be - according to management analysis - at the value-based ("break-point"-analysis) equilibrium. This is the case at the "break-even-point". Thus, to realize a total equilibrium, all market participants should be at the "break-even-point" (value-based equilibrium) and the supply- and demand quantity should be equal (quantity-based equilibrium). From this viewpoint, equilibria have been demonstrated by Keynes just as partial and thus highly special equilibria unable to prevent economic crises. Particularly serious is also the failure observing our own criticism on the quantity theory. Also in his

---

[39] See Leijonhufvud, A.: On Keynesian Economics and the Economics of Keynes, New York a.o. 1968, pp. 49 ff. (German: Über Keynes und den Keynesianismus, Köln 1973, p. 32 ff.); see also Johnson, H.: Neue Entwicklungen in der Geldtheorie ..., p. 31

[40] See Johnson, H.: Neue Entwicklungen in der Geldtheorie ..., p. 31

[41] See Johnson, H.: Neue Entwicklungen in der Geldtheorie ..., p. 31

approach, prices are independent from supply- and demand quantities or rather elasticity, but from liquidity preferences. Thus, above all occurring disequilibria in practice have also led to renewed changes in monetary policies on the neo-quantity theory and neo-quantity policy.

However, criticism has also begun at this old critical issue. An approach of general criticism regarding contradiction in formulating price dependencies has not followed yet. Prices are independent in the neo-quantity theory of supply- respectively demand quantity respectively appropriate elasticity. Thus, the neo-quantity theory stands in the same contradiction to basic findings in the economy. In addition, the neo-quantity theory is unable to avoid disequilibria in practice. This fact is valid, even though causes of equilibria on money-, goods-, and labor markets have been stated.[42] For the creation of equilibria on the goods- and labor markets, special assumptions are necessary because the Fisher Exchange Equation and also its modern variants just create equilibria of money supplies and money demands. Consequently, just a partial and special equilibrium of all three markets is available. Additionally, it has to be proven whether the Fisher Equation of Exchange and its modern variants have – after all - created money- and goods market equilibrium. However, not only practical experience has been revoking it. Equations - considering money velocities - do not present equations of equality but of inequality.

Not only must the values be equal but also the units of measurements. Multiplications in money units (for example euro or US-dollar) measured in money supplies with a velocity, measured by path or distance per time does not present a useful unit of measurement. The result is - for example - euro times path per time units. This definitely still remains an unknown measurement unit. Whether this measurement unit is useful – is still to be discussed. It probably does not make any sense at all. The situation is different on the right side of the equation. Exchange quantity or similar referred to items, such as gross national-, gross domestic product, and national income are measured in money units (i.e. euro or US-Dollar). However, multiplying with price levels, indexes without measurement units, yield the measurement unit: money (i.e. euro or US-Dollar). This makes sense. However, it is not equal from the measurement unit on the left side of the equation. Consequently, an inequality is achieved, thereby documenting inequalities.

Principally, the presented problem can be adjusted, if the velocity of money is applied with the cash coefficient. A coefficient does not have - just as the price level - a measurement unit. However, cash coefficients cannot be defined as re-

---

[42] See i.e. Monissen, H.G.: Die relative Stabilität von Kreislaufgeschwindigkeit des Geldes und Investitionsmultiplikator: Eine Zusammenfassung der Diskussion; in: Brunner, K./Monissen, H.G./Neumann, M.J.M (Ed.): Geldtheorie, Köln 1974, pp. 267 – 289, here p. 271 f.; Tobin, J.: Ein Allgemeiner Gleichgewichtsansatz zur Geldtheorie, in: Brunner, K./Monissen, H.G./Neumann, M.J.M (Ed.): Geldtheorie, Köln 1974, pp. 219 – 234

ciprocal values of money velocities (1 divided by velocity of money). Then the problem has just been replaced to another level.

Otherwise, it can be assumed that the velocity of money has not at all been intended, but that it had only been created by misinterpreting relations. This argument has been supported by calculation examples of Mankiw/Taylor.[43] In following Mankiw/Taylor one gets the notion that the term turnover rate would preferably meet the definition better than the term velocity of money. Cash coefficient would then be better interpreted as money turnover rate resistance. Cassel[44] has more clearly described the misinterpretation of turnover resistance. He has criticized the term of not having been defined properly. His definition assumed all coins having the same frequencies in their application for all purchases in one individual specified economic period. Thus, money velocity for each individual coin is the number of payments achieved for each coin in an economic period.

Finally, the suggestion for improvement should be introduced – formulating a third equation for securing equilibria on labor markets.

The liquidity theory distinguishes itself from all other money theoretical approaches, only by justifying a deviant control parameter - liquidity. Discussed are alternative deferrals or rather definitions of liquidity. Up to now, none of the followers of this theory has been able to work out any definitions of monetary policy control mechanisms. Achievements of equilibria have neither theoretically nor practically been successful.

All three monetary theories distinguish themselves by receiving general criticisms regarding control options or rather control abilities of economic processes. Difficulty to determine previous (forecast issue) money supplies to be introduced into market cycles in time, independently selected control parameters (selection parameters) and its (production- and transport- or rather distribution issues) processing of all desired exchange actions by central banks. Regarding presented issues, there is just one solution possible. Application of security factors is a must. Impacts are always too high when difficulties have occurred and it is also possible that money supplies have been introduced too early into the cycle. Negative impacts have been sufficiently described in money, theoretical- and political literature. The result is inflation with undesired effects on economic processes. However preventing this, is exactly the utmost objective of monetary policies.

A second general critical issue is that the three approaches of the monetary theory are unable to strive for total equilibria. For that purpose, the Fisher Exchange Equation respectively, its variants would have to be extended explicitly, consid-

---

[43] See Mankiw, N.G./Taylor, M.P.: Grundzüge der Volkswirtschaftslehre, 4th ed., Stuttgart 2008, p. 742

[44] See Cassel, G.: Theoretische Sozialökonomie, 6th ed., Darmstadt 1968 (Leipzig 1918[1]), p. 401

ering goods- and labor markets. However, this has only been successful in theory. In practice, this has not occurred yet – disequilibria and crisis have been occurring.

Finally, it is necessary to consider, whether there are contradictions and thus, efficiency complications resulting by mixing ("policy-mix") the three approaches of monetary theories, performed by central banks. It would be possible to explain avoidable disequilibria or rather crisis in practice. However, if there are no effective complications of approaches present, then they could be referred to as achievements of mutual equilibria. Practice documents with constant appearing crisis show that approaches are unable to create equilibria. This might be due to demonstrated general inabilities, creating monetary policies with total equilibria. The issue remains, whether there are any effective complications left. Research has shown that there are effective complications. Research carried out by Friedman has proven that there are time lags.[45] Time lags have led to delayed impacts of interest rate changes influencing economic processes – however, influences occur when opposite desired results have become necessary. Since the effect of change of money supplies respectively liquidity is considerable quicker, interest rate controls respectively liquidity contradict interest rate controls and money amount controls as well as liquidity controls. This is at least valid for the parts of liquidity of non-interest independent rates. For the interest rate related part, liquidity is a contradiction of money amount controls to be concluded.

[45] See Friedman, M.: A Program for Monetary Stability, pp. 189 – 203, Friedman, M.: The Lag in Effect of Monetary Policy, pp. 447 – 466

Part 2: Functions of Money respectively Euro

Anticipating money functions is essential for examining the security of the euro after the discussion of the monetary system and its basic theoretical influence on economic processes as well as controlling money respectively monetary policy function possibilities have taken place.[46] Money functions can be applied as evaluation criteria proving whether or not the euro is a secure currency.

1. Money, Additional Good to Exchange other Goods

Money - as it has generally been acknowledged – has one disadvantage - it is not edible! This old, wise saying of the Cree-Indians has become very familiar throughout environmental policies. Actually, the saying is correct, however, it is inappropriate for the situation. Money must not be eaten. Money is an additional good that has been proven suboptimal throughout history. Money permits achieving exchanges in an optimal method.[47] Thus, goods are exchanged for money - in a monetary economy. Money buys edible and non-edible goods. This particular task is - without doubt – better than any other exchange goods. Thus, money is an exchange good. It can take on different forms.[48] Latest developed form is – probably - plastic money.

2. Euro, Currency in European Monetary Union and Functions

Three functions have been assigned to the monetary theory,[49] defining further the function of just only serving as a pure exchange-medium. Those three functions are: calculation unit function, (2) bilateral interaction, and (3) store-of-value function.

The following chapter demonstrates changes of awareness and behavior in the perception of the three functions of citizens after removing "deutschmark" and introducing euros.

---

[46] See the definition, functions of money, and how it is generated and how it affects the economy i.e. Sauernheimer, K.: Vom Gelde, in: Review of Economics, Vol. 61 (2010), pp. 279 - 299

[47] See advantages of money usage Kath, D.: Geld und Kredit, in: Vahlens Kompendium der Wirtschaftstheorie und Wirtschaftspolitik, Vol. 1., 2nd ed., München 1994, pp. 173 – 214, here pp. 178 - 180

[48] See for the forms of money i.e. Kath, D.: Geld und Kredit, pp. 176 f.

[49] See Brunner, K./Meltzer, A.H.: Die Verwendung von Geld: Geld in der Theorie einer Tauschwirtschaft, in: Brunner, K./Monissen, H.G./Neumann, M.J.M (Ed.): Geldtheorie, Köln 1974, pp. 50 – 73, here p. 50

2.1 Euro as Accounting Unit

Accounting units for the former dm (above) and the euro (below) are demonstrated in fig. 3. It shows that there have not been any changes regarding calculation units by introducing the new currency euro. The old and the new currencies are taken down on a scale between 'zero' and 'hundred'. One euro is subdivided in 100 euro-cent.

Fig. 3: Comparison of dm and euro regarding arithmetic unit functions

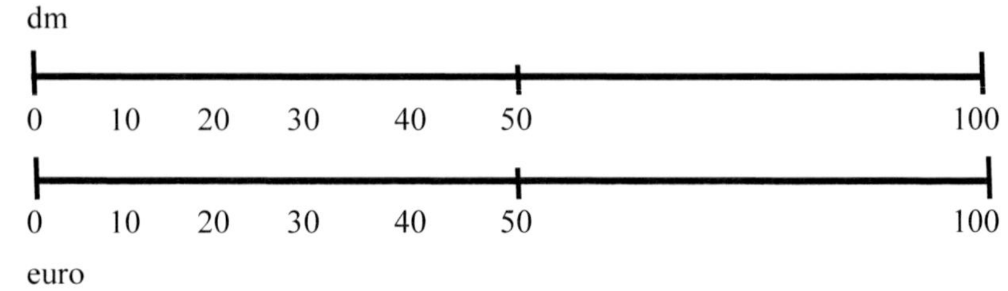

Source: own demonstration

Equality of the former and new currency simplifies the calculation with the new currency. People of today do not need to rethink this particular matter.

2.2 Euro, an Exchange-Medium

Figure 4 shows the scaling of currencies dm (above) and euro (below) as exchange-media.

Fig. 4: Comparison of dm and euro regarding the medium of exchange

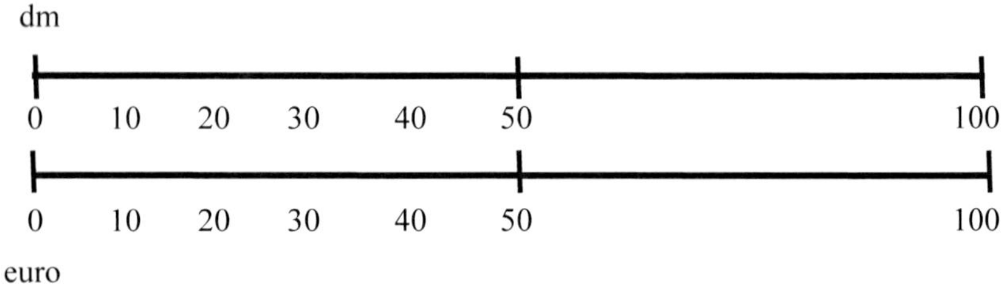

Source: own demonstration

Clarified is the usage of the same scaling between 'zero' and 'one hundred' just as for the calculation unit function. Considering exchange medium function, citizens, also, do not have to rethink.

2.3 Euro as a Store-of-Value Medium

Finally, dm and euro are compared against each other, regarding the store-of-value function. Comparison is presented in fig. 5.

Fig: 5: Comparison of dm and euro regarding the store-of-value function

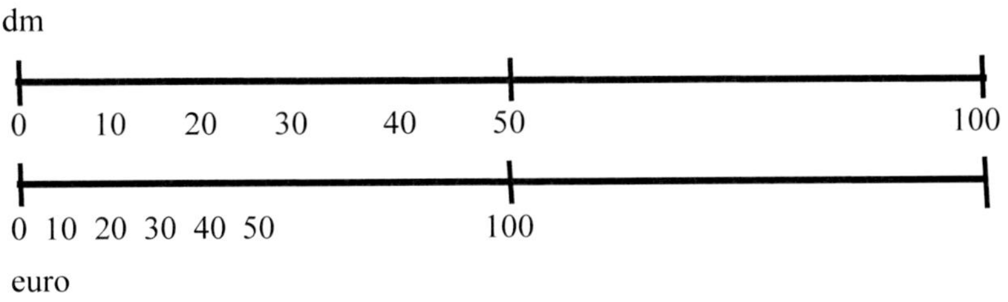

Source: own demonstration

The taken down scaling for the dm (above) and the euro (below) just clarify a relative similarity regarding store-of-value functions of both currencies. Actually, scaled for both currencies between 'zero' and 'hundred'; however, spacing between scaling values respectively scale-units is a different one. This is obtained by exchange-rates of currencies. Two dm are roughly calculated with 100 Pfennige or 50 euro-cents. This conversion of currencies just takes place in calculation values. Citizens, generally have – as we know today – a spending behavior – one euro equalizes one dm. Sellers have exploited this psychological and habitual effect and thus have converted many prices from one dm to one euro instead of 50 euro-cent. For this reason, the relationship of both currencies is presented in fig. 5, regarding store-of-value functions, the scale for the euro has been changed, so that the value scale for the dm one dm represents only 50 Pfennige. For products, buyers pay one euro today – formerly, they would have just paid 50 Pfennige.

2.4 Compliance of Money Functions with Euro

Evaluation of the euro regarding the compliance with money functions is positive. The euro complies exactly, just as the former dm has done, with the three functions of money. Regarding calculation unit- and exchange-rate functions in comparison to the dm, a difference has not been noted yet. However, the store-of-value function shows a difference in scaling. As a result, the store-of-value function does not influence the euro at all. However, there is one psychological habitual behavioral issue. Citizens are unable to work (always) because they are calculating according to former scaling. However, these cause issues to be interpreted in the following chapter. Furthermore, impacts are to be discussed.

3. Evaluations of Euro

Evaluations of the euro have come about relatively quickly in different media after its introduction. The euro has been described as "teuro". In other words, euro has also been described as an accelerator. Both descriptions of the euro are to be explicitly clarified and justified. Additionally, impacts of the euro on possible existing equilibria are to be examined.

3.1 Euro as "teuro"

Every member state of the European Union had had to determine its exchange-rate according to its former currency, before it introduced the euro. By means of these particular exchange-rates, all have been calculated in their former identified exchange-rates. This process is surely logical and also makes sense. Assumed is that established validity of value ratios of former currencies have been complied with. Thus, not a single citizen should have been off worse or better than before the currency change had been achieved. However, unfortunately - in practice - this has never been the case – former value ratios have never been complied with. Practice has demonstrated that in conversion of values, determined value ratios have not been maintained. The principle of shrewdness has led to the fact that prices have not stayed at a constant level. After a short time, the selected prices have increased "inflation hedged", at about one hundred percent in the Federal Republic of Germany.[50] However, neither pensions nor income from financial assets have been improved. Especially striking features have been price increases with cheap products, products priced one "Deutsche Mark" and directly after the currency changeover, priced one euro. Price increases with expensive products have also occurred. Well-known, have also been – above all – price increases in catering trades. According to the principle, shrewdness - sellers have taken advantage of a psychological effect. They have developed confidence in the effect that the majority of citizens - at least - would spend the coins in the new currency – just as they have been used to do, beforehand. One euro has been equalized to one "Deutsche Mark" (dm). Consequently, one euro has been spent in value units equal to one dm. Increase of selected prices of one hundred percent and exploiting the mentioned psychological impacts, have thus led to the commonly known nickname "teuro" for the euro. This "expensive" impact is presented in fig. 6.

[50] A price increase of one hundred percent is discussed in a simplified method. Assumed is one euro equal to two „deutschmark". According to the applied exchange rate one euro had a value of 1.9853 „deutschmark". Thus, the price increase was only 98.53 percent.

Fig. 6: Impact of euro on wages and selected prices (in percentage)

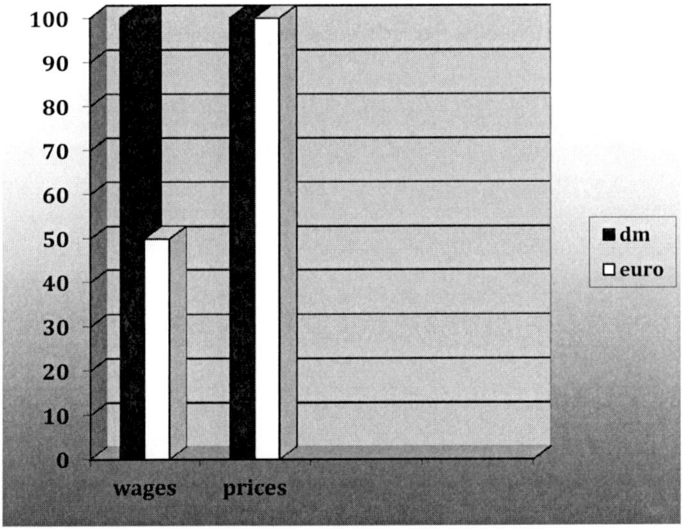

Source: own presentation

The nickname "teuro" is no longer significant in today's media nor is it in any way popular, as it had happened directly after the euro introduction. However, the above described impact of the euro is still occurring nowadays. Increase of prices has not been occurring in one step to one hundred percent, but increase has been actually slowed down throughout many years. However, one could observe considerable higher prices today compared to 2001. The impact of price increases, first noticed with selected products, can be perceived with almost all products. Assumed is, impacts become slowly more and more identifiable with higher priced products. One effect, beginning at first with cheap products and then slowly creeping up to higher priced products has been observed. The impact is graphically demonstrated in fig. 7. In the year 2001 impacts appeared only for cheap products. In the year 2014 impacts on products have already been presented at considerable higher prices. Fig. 7 demonstrates normative products at prices up to 12,000 euro. The impact to even still higher priced products has been expanding. Finally, even the most expensive products demonstrate a one hundred percent price increase, compared to the year 2001. Thus, the euro has definitely been known for a long time as "teuro".

Fig. 7: Impact of euro on the selected prices (2001 - 2014)

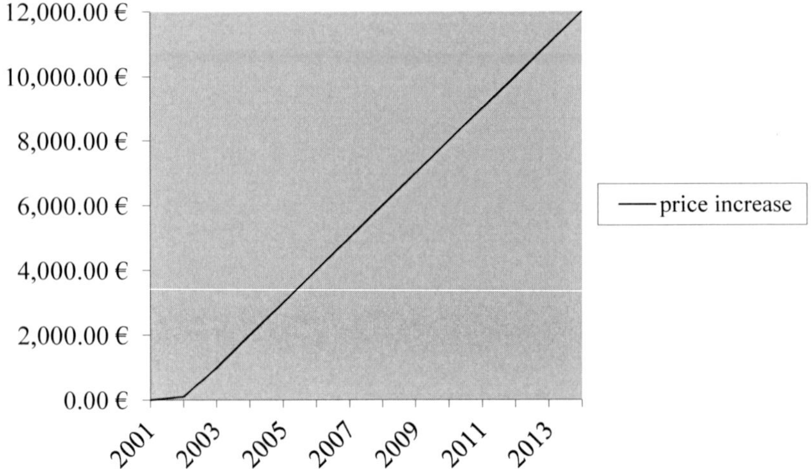

Source: own presentation

The long term rise in price impact of the euro has been different to the short termed excursive rise in price impact - not inflation-hedged. Prices for almost all products have been traditionally increased every year. Price increases have been considerably higher since the introduction of the euro. Had prices been raised by just one “Deutsche Mark” before the euro introduction, they would have been increased by one euro after the euro introduction had taken place. Again, the psychological effect plays a defined role – just equalizing the “Deutsche Mark” with one euro.

However, income strata have not all been affected equally regarding price increases. The higher the income the less affect with price increases for involved persons. The higher the income the less is the effect of life conditions caused by price increases.

Fig. 8: Influence of the euro depending on incomes

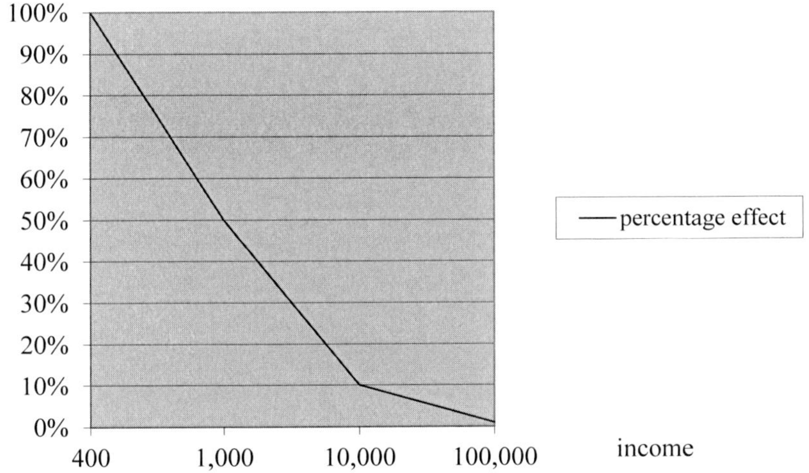

Source: own presentation

Price increases and thus their impacts, also depend on competition intensities on markets (compare fig. 9). Companies are able to enforce price increases easiest at zero competition intensities (compare fig. 9). There are hardly any respectively no competitors at all (monopolistic situation) taking advantages from competitions by participating in price increases.

Price increases at a competition intensity at 'one' will not be possible (polypolistic situation). Many competitors do not participate in price increases, so that demands would be lost for companies increasing their prices - they would become bankrupt.

The presented impairment curve of citizens caused by price increases presented in competition dependencies in fig. 9 is normative. Impairments at competition intensities are 'zero' at a minimum – this is logical. Maximum impairments at competition intensity 'one' is also logical.

Fig. 9: Influence of the euro depending on competitive intensity levels

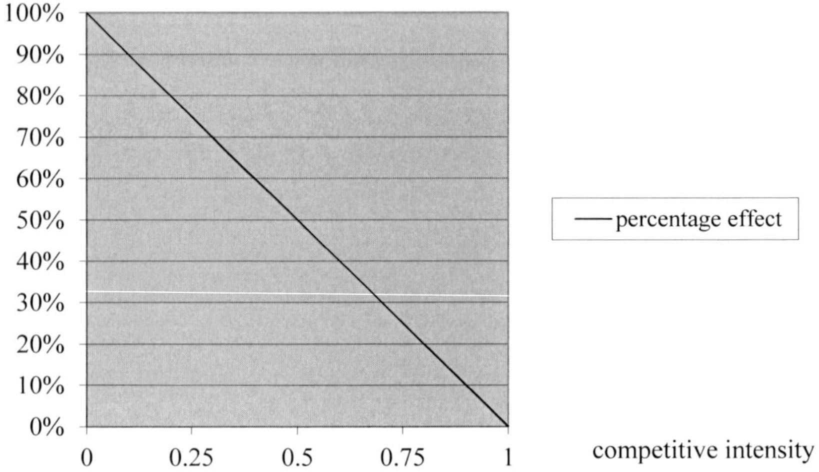

Source: own presentation

Furthermore, citizen impairment caused by companies increasing their prices at euro introduction time depends on demand price elasticity. Demand price elasticity is between 'zero' and 'infinite'. Assumed is a price elasticity of 10,000 up to zero in fig. 10. Demand reacts on a price elasticity of 10,000 considerably on price changes, thus, companies increasing their prices would lose all of their demands. Consequently, there would not be any price increase achieved. Thus, citizen economic situation impairments would turn out to be zero. With decreasing price elasticity demands of companies increasing their prices would lose fewer demands. Consequently, price increases are enforceable. Consequently, citizen impairments of the economic situation caused by price increases are rising to one hundred percent at a demand price elasticity at 'zero'.

The proportional impairment presented in fig. 10 is normative. The curve has been derived from the logic of connections.

Connections presented in fig. 9 and 10 show that price increases of the euro have not been able to be enforced for all goods at the same extent. The described psychological impact at the euro introduction could not be utilized equally. Demand price elasticity and intensity of competition elasticity have prevented it.

Fig. 10: Influence of the euro depending on the level of the price elasticity of demand

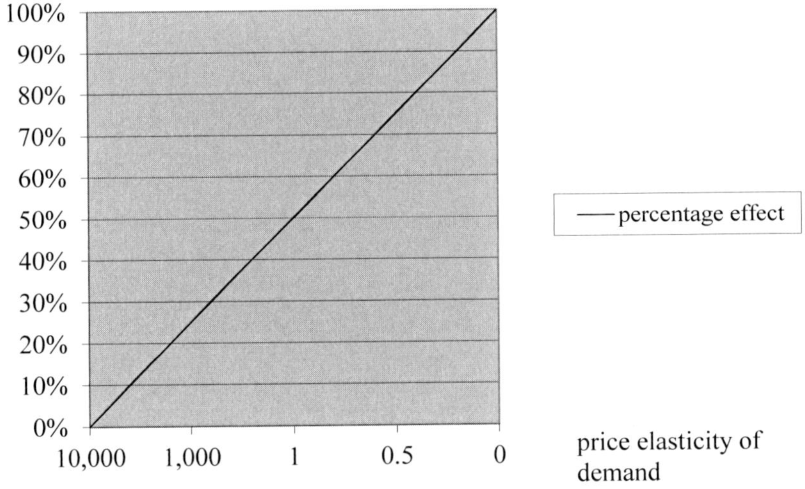

Source; own presentation

3.2 Euro, an Accelerator

The euro, having already been called "teuro" at its introduction, has also been an accelerator. Since many prices have been increased by one hundred percent – but not - the wages – many citizens have therefore, spent more money quicker than before the euro introduction had taken place. Bill folds or respectively cash registers have been emptied quicker.

This particular accelerator impact depends on one hand on the height of provided incomes respectively, assets. Otherwise, impacts depend on price increases. Again, these depend on market situations, especially on price elasticity demands and competition intensities.

The accelerator impact has not only exerted the mentioned individual economic impacts. But also from the macroeconomic viewpoint, euro-crisis, have been caused quicker than before the introduction.

The accelerator impact of the euro on an individual- and macroeconomic level depends on the exchange-rate of the euro to the former currency. A 1:1 ratio can be seen as ideal from this viewpoint.[51] Regarding the value storing function,

[51] This "ideal" exchange rate in a Monetary Community respectively - Union is only possible to achieve for one state. This specified state would have great advantages compared with oth-

there is neither a psychological impact, nor cause of a price increase, nor an acceleration taking place. Value ratios remain stable.

Tab. 2: Accelerating effect of the euro depending on the exchange-rate to the old currency

1:1	=	no acceleration
1:2	=	minor acceleration
1:12	=	higher acceleration

Source: own presentation

A small acceleration can still be observed at an exchange-rate of 1:2. However, exchange-rates of 1:12 have a considerable higher acceleration rate, because value-storing functions have reached greater psychological effects.

Due to accelerating effect dependencies of provided incomes, respectively assets, results are - small cash bill folds have been emptied quicker than bigger ones. Consequently, in a country with small available cash, crisis will appear sooner than in ones with a lot of cash.

Furthermore, one can observe, that cash is being emptied at a faster rate, if it is impossible to equalize income sides for increased expenditures. Consequently, accelerating effects appear sooner and more intensified in countries with many wage-dependent employees, based on wage-management without compensation possibilities, than in a country with many employees, because of their independent position possessing compensation possibilities.

3.3 Impact of Introduction of Euro on Existing Equilibria

However, the euro is not only the "teuro" and accelerator. It is also a destroyer of existing equilibria. Assumed is that an economic unit has been, at the time of the euro introduction at an equilibrium (income = expenditures), then the euro introduction has destroyed the equilibrium. This particular impact of the euro exerted on equilibria can easily be explained with a simple calculation example. Assumed is an economic unit with assets of 1,000 euros - before the euro introduction - income at a level of 1,000 dm and expenditures of 1,000 dm. Thus a financial equilibrium has been achieved. Income was equal to expenditures. Should economic units have been applied to the income from working relationships (wages) at the exchange-rate of 1:2 on euro introduction day (1 euro = 2 dm), income would have been fixed at an exchange-rate of 1:2 (1 euro = 2 dm). At the same time, expenditures have been converted with exchange-rates. Thus, expenditures have also been determined at 500 euros. Because product prices have doubled on euro introduction day, results on the expenditure column had

---

er member states. Thus, it is appropriate not to use the "ideal" exchange rate for any of the member states.

indeed an exchange-rate of 1:1. Thus the economic unit had at an income of 500 euro and expenditures at the level of 1,000 euro. Financial equilibria, before the introduction, do not exist any longer. In conclusion - the euro has destroyed existing equilibria.

Otherwise, examples could also be constructed where euros have led to equilibria. Assumed is an economic unit at the level of 2,000 dm and expenditures at the level of 1,000 dm before the euro introduction had taken place, an income of 2,000 dm and expenditures of 1,000 dm. A financial equilibrium did not exist. With the euro introduction, income and expenditures at the level of 1,000 euros have been achieved (500 euro resulting from the conversion and 500 euro from the price increase). Thus, the euro introduction has achieved a financial equilibrium.

It is difficult to say, whether the euro introduction has led to more financial disequilibria or equilibria. Both could be theoretically possible. However, there has been the justified assumption that a low income (employees) has destroyed financial equilibria very often respectively strengthened disequilibria.

Part 3: Conditions for Monetary Security

Conditions for currencies to be secure have been presented in literature. Three conditions have been listed. These conditions are listed quickly. Currencies must be

- stable,
- neutral, and
- forgery-proof.

If all three conditions for a currency are achieved, it is known as a secure currency. Responsibility of competent issue- respectively central banks is to guarantee achieving these three conditions and therefore securities of currencies. Thus, the European System of Central Banks with the European Central Bank at the top is responsible for the security of the euro.[1]

The three conditions for currency security are to be discussed in the following chapter.

1. Money Value Stability

First condition for guaranteeing security is currency stability. The term stability is more precisely described with money stability – in other words, money will not lose its value. Thus, the store-of-value function has been achieved by one hundred percent. If inflation or deflation is not present, a currency is stable. Additionally to the term money stability, the term price stability is used.

Requirement for money stability for the Federal Republic of Germany is determined in § 1 of the law for the promotion of stability and growth of the economy (StabWG).[2] This specified legislation discusses price level stability.

Formulations of the law of the promotion of stability and growth of economy are based on Art. 109 Constitution (GG).[3] According to Art. 109 (2) federal and regional state (in their state budget) requirements of macro-economic equilibria have to be observed. Thus, promoting stability and growth of the economy has still determined three further objectives. These are guaranteeing high employment level (full employment), steady and reasonable growth, and an external

---

[1] See Vertrag über die Europäische Union ..., 3. Protokoll über die Satzung des Europäischen Systems der Zentralbanken und der Europäischen Zentralbank

[2] See Gesetz zur Förderung der Stabilität und des Wachstums der Wirtschaft (StabWG) vom 8. Juni 1967 (BGBl. I p. 582), das zuletzt durch Artikel 135 der Verordnung vom 31. Oktober 2006 (BGBl. I p. 2407) geändert worden ist

[3] See Grundgesetz für die Bundesrepublik Deutschland vom 23. Mai 1949 (BGBl. p. 1) BGBl. III 100-1

equilibrium as well. Discussed is in this specified connection with the additional price level stability of a "magic square".

Disadvantage of these legal formulations is that the term macro-economic equilibrium is diluted down by a "weak" interpretation through practical policies. Consequences caused by deviations of equilibria resulting in practice are not taken seriously. It should be clearly stressed that crisis can only be avoided by maintaining strictly exact equilibria. Every single deviation from the equilibrium causes irreparable damage to disequilibria and thus one step further to a crisis.

"Weak" target achievement agreement interpretation degrees of law promoted stability and determined objective growth should only be shown at price level stability. Stability and growth promotion of determined objectives should just demonstrate price level stability at destinations. Price stability is only possible when there is no deviation in equilibrium present. A deviation of one percent is noted as achieving objectives of price level stability. However, there have also been years in which considerable higher deviations have been tolerated (i.e. 1981 6.3%, 1982 5.2%, 1992 5.1%, and 1993 4.5%).[4] Additionally, a contradiction in legal formulation is observed. This contradiction is based on the requirement of a steady and reasonable growth destroying an (macro-economic) equilibrium. Just balanced growth can guarantee persistence of equilibria respectively transfers into new equilibria. However, an open issue remains, whether or not - and how balanced growths can be achieved. The sure way to maintain a macro-economic equilibrium is maintaining a "zero-growth respectively stagnation."

Furthermore, stability requirements are determined in the Federal Bank Law (BbankG).[5] The Deutsche Bundesbank is responsible to guarantee the price stability (§ 3 BbankG). Additionally, the Deutsche Bundesbank has to support the economic policy of the Federal Government (§ 12 BbankG). Thus the Federal Government is responsible to implement the law to promote the stability and growth of the economy with four objectives to guarantee the objective price level stability supported by the Deutsche Bundesbank.

On supra national level, the European Union, stability requirement has been fixed as the objective of the European Monetary Union respectively as objective of the European System of Central Banks (ESCB) in Art. 105 of the Treaty Establishing the European Community[6] and determined Art. 2 of the 3. Protocol to the Treaty on European Union.[7] Priority objective of the ESCB is guaranteeing price stability in supporting the general economic policies in the Community/Union.

---

[4] See Annex 3, Tab. 28

[5] See Gesetz über die Deutsche Bundesbank (BbankG) vom 26.7. 1957 in der Fassung vom 22.10.1992 (BGBl. I, p. 1782)

[6] See Art. 105 Vertrag zur Gründung der Europäischen Gemeinschaft …

[7] See Vertrag über die Europäische Union …, 3. Protokoll über die Satzung des Europäischen Systems der Zentralbanken und der Europäischen Zentralbank, Art. 2

Theoretic foundation of stability requirement can be derived from money amount controls based on the Fisher Equation of Exchange respectively modern variants of this equation. This will be discussed in a later chapter (compare Part 6, 2.).

2. Money Neutrality

Second condition for guaranteeing the security of a currency respectively money has been represented in theory in many contributions. This second condition is money neutrality represented – above all – by the quantity- and cash management theoreticians. David Hume[8] (1752) saw the theory of neutral money in the year 1752. Unfortunately, this particular condition of money – as far as it can be evaluated by externals – has not been considered or taken note of in money- and currency policies. This statement can be derived,[9] among other multiple suggestions; on part of policies for the solution of the euro-crisis.[10] Suggestions creating euro neutrality is thus far unknown.

Controversially discussed in economic literature is money neutrality. Relationship between stability and money neutrality has also been evaluated differently.

Wicksell has considered an identity for conditions for stability and neutrality.[11] Other authors have rejected the identity of stability- and neutrality conditions[12] as well as money neutrality in equilibrium of the perfect competition. Since neutral money does not dominate, it becomes the disruptive factor of equilibria.[13] Disadvantages of this viewpoint are discussions to money neutrality, just as discussions of perfect competition have been carried out – they have not been seen as being practice relevant because conditions of the perfect competition have ranked as rigid respectively impractical. Consequently, stability conditions in practical monetary policies have been dominant and neutrality conditions have been neglected.

---

[8] See Hume, D.: Political Discourses, Edinburgh 1752 (reproduction London 2015, pp. 27 – 39, esp. p. 27)

[9] See also Duczynski, P.: On the Empirics of Non-Neutrality of Money: Cross-Country Evidence, in: Indian Economic Review, New Series, Vol. 43 (2008), pp. 1 - 15

[10] See Shambaugh, J.C./Reis, R./Rey, H.: The Euro´s Three Crises, in: Brookings Papers on Economic Activity, Spring 2012, pp. 157 – 231; Clairmont, F.F.: The Euro Crash, in: Economic and Political Weekly, Vol. 35 (2000), pp. 3644 - 3646

[11] See Wicksell, K.: Geldzins und Güterpreis, p. 130

[12] See for discussion: Wagner, H.-J.: Stabiles oder neutrales Geld: Eine ordnungspolitische Diskussion, in: Neuere Entwicklungen in der Geldtheorie und Geldpolitik, ed. by Bofinger, P./Ketterer, K.-H., Tübingen 1996, pp. 71 – 90, here pp. 74 – 78, 83 - 87

[13] See Wagner, H.-J.: Stabiles oder neutrales Geld …, p. 85

Money neutrality has been achieved according to Newlyn,[14] when money does not have any influence on prices respectively credit markets.[15] Friedman and Schwartz have discussed and defined money neutrality - just as cash (according to Newlyn). Under certain conditions, also central bank money can be neutral. However, to verify neutrality of central bank money appropriate interpretations of some transactions have become necessary.[16] Additionally, the definition of neutrality has also been independent from the definitions of money.[17]

The term neutral money (money neutrality) has usually been led back into literature to Wicksell. The Swedish economist Wicksell has been seen as the creator of both terms "neutral" and "value stable" money. According to Wicksell, money is neutral, whenever the value of money meets the terms with the value of the natural rate. The rate is natural when the real return is equal to the capital in production. Natural rates guarantee price level stability or maintain values of real money.[18]

v. Hayek has also been concerned intensively with money neutrality. According to Hayek, there must be three conditions met for money neutrality: (1) money quantity must not have any influence on the real macro-economic factors (quantitative neutrality). (2) Money must not have any influence on timely preferences of economic entities (time neutrality) and (3) money must not have any influence on primary distributions of national income (distributional neutrality). Meeting these three conditions, money domains do not have any influence on goods spheres and money - it is consequently neutral.[19]

Huppert has discussed other conditions from the viewpoint of an act of exchange for neutrality, other conditions from the viewpoint of an act of exchange for money neutrality used for processes of exchange acts. He lists the following five conditions: (1) principle of subsidiary, (2) continuation principle, (3) mainte-

---

[14] See Newlyn, W.T.: Theory of Money, 2nd ed., Oxford 1971 (1962[1]), pp. 36 f.; see older and different definitions and discussions of the neutrality of money i.e. Egle, W.: Das neutrale Geld, Jena 1933, esp. pp. V, 1 ff., 80 ff.

[15] See Newlyn, W.T.: The Definition of Money: Net Wealth and Neutrality as Criteria: Reply, in: Journal of Money, Credit and Banking, Vol. 4 (1972), pp. 118 – 120, here p. 118; see also Negishi, T.: Conditions for Neutral Money, in: The Review of Economic Studies, Vol. 31 (1964), pp. 147 - 148

[16] See Friedman, M./Schwartz, A.: Die Definition des Geldes: Nettovermögen und Neutralität als Kriterium, in: Brunner, K./Monissen, H.G./Neumann, M.J.M (Ed.): Geldtheorie, Köln 1974, pp. 74 – 90, here p. 83

[17] See neutrality of money also Johnson, H.: Neue Entwicklungen in der Geldtheorie ..., pp. 30 – 34 and quoted literature

[18] See Wicksell, K.: Geldzins und Güterpreis, p. 130

[19] See Hayek, F.v.: Über „neutrales Geld", in: Zeitschrift für Nationalökonomie, Vol. 4 (1933), pp. 659 – 661; for the definition of neutral money see Hayek, F.A.: Geldtheorie und Konjunkturtheorie, Wien, Leipzig 1929, p. 59

nance of exchange processes, (4) principle of revolving changes, and remuneration principles.[20]

Presenting neutrality of money as conditions for a secure currency, significant opinions of Keynes must not be left out. This shall also apply by not discussing all other great economists, expressing their views on this particular topic. It should be sufficient, just referring to the mentioned quoted literature.

Keynes has derived money stability from interest rates. In his work "from money"[21] he has discussed natural interest rates used as continuation and clarification of terms of "natural interest rates" that have formerly been used by Wicksell. Continuation has been necessary because the natural interest rate defined by Keynes, according to the natural interest rate defined by Wicksell, to guarantee stability of not clearly defined price levels. Keynes has defined interest rate as natural interest rate securing the equality of saving (S) and investment (I) (S = I).[22] Keynes has detached himself in the "General Theory" from his first definition of natural interest rates. Now he defines a 'neutral interest'. He clarifies in a footnote that this definition is not compatible with the "General Theory" definitions of neutral money by other authors. Furthermore, Keynes adds that the term optimum interest rate would meet the objective better. Neutral interest rates are at the equilibrium stage by a constellation of production and employment to elasticity of the total employment leading to zero.[23]

In literature it is not only the definition of neutrality of money being discussed controversially, but also the question whether it is possible to achieve neutral money in a real economy.

Three arguments are discussed against achievement of neutral money in a real economy, result from the fact that neutral money cannot produce any interest. The arguments are:[24] (1) no more savings without interest, (2) not enough capital without interest, (3) an indefinite quantity of credit is being raised.

The first argument is regarding the currently achieved monetary system absolutely true. However, would a macro-economic equilibrium be actualized, saving would be on one side impossible, and on the other side unnecessary. The first argument can then only be partially applied toward the realization of neutral money. The same is true for the second argument. Assumed is insufficient capital in case of unavailable interest in a real monetary system. However, this is not

---

[20] See Huppert, W.: Neutralität des Geldes, in: Finanzarchiv, Neue Serie, Vol. 4 (1937), pp. 452 – 475, here pp. 455 f.

[21] See Keynes, J.M.: Vom Gelde, 3rd ed., Berlin 1983, pp. 127, 160 f.

[22] See Keynes, J.M.: Allgemeine Theorie ..., p. 204

[23] See Keynes, J.M.: Allgemeine Theorie ..., pp. 204 f.

[24] See Suhr, D.: Geld ohne Mehrwert. Entlastung der Marktwirtschaft von monetären Transaktionskosten, Frankfurt/M. 1983, p. 78; Suhr, D.: The Capitalistic Cost-Benefit Structure of Money. An Analysis of Money´s Structural Nonneutrality and its Effects on the Economy, Berlin, Heidelberg, New York a.o. 1989, esp. pp. 110 ff., 117 - 122

the case at an equilibrium situation. The third argument cannot be seen as convincing at all. It contravenes the second argument. Should there be not enough capital available, then a credit cannot be taken out indefinitely.

Rugina has expressed himself to achieve the possibility for neutralizing money.[25] This was contradicted by Meyer.[26] Meyer actually assumes neutral money to be possible but not in a real monetary system. It should actually be clear, that the currently applied real monetary system does not enable the possibility to achieve real money. An economy without any interest is only possible in an equilibrium situation. Equilibrium does not only make neutral money available but it also protects for economic crisis. In case that an achievement of a (macro-economic) equilibrium can be shown under practical conditions, then neutral money can also be achieved. Thus, the renunciation could then be gotten over. However, it should not be misjudged that the consequences of this process are restructuring of the current money- and economic system. Arguments for this procedure can surely be derived from the former realized prohibition of interest earnings.[27] Necessity to change the real monetary- and economic system to achieve neutral money results also from the Friedman and Schwartz met statements, that according to the definition of Newlyn, only cash and (at a stricter interpretation) also central bank money are neutral.[28]

2.1 Discussion about Money Neutrality

Second condition for currency security, money neutrality has been demanded by many authors as well as refused by many.[29] Especially members of the Austrian School (among Haberler) are known for rejecting money neutrality. Assumed is money influencing goods prices and goods quantities. Streissler argues that Hayek had observed money neutrality as an ideal goal of monetary policies of a central bank, but not as a necessary success of action.[30] Streissler has described himself as "Belächler der Ammenmärchen von der Exogenität und Neutalität des Geldes (smile greeter at old wife's tale of exogeneity and money neutrali-

---

[25] See Rugina, A.: Geldtypen und Geldordnungen. Fundamente für eine echte allgemeine Geld- und Wirtschaftstheorie, Stuttgart, Köln 1949, pp. 210 - 217; Rugina, A.: Und es kann doch „neutrales" Geld geben! In: Weltwirtschaftliches Archiv, Vol. 67 (1953), pp. 57 - 68

[26] See Meyer, F.W.: „Natürliches" Geld? In: Weltwirtschaftliches Archiv, Vol. 64 (1950), pp. 1 - 11; Meyer, F.W.: „Neutrales" Geld ist denkbar – aber nicht in einer „natürlichen" Geldordnung, in: Weltwirtschaftliches Archiv, Vol. 67 (1953), S. 68 – 73, esp. p. 71

[27] See interest rate prohibition i.e. Witte, H.: Die nachhaltige Marktwirtschaft, p. 65 and quoted literature

[28] See Friedman, M./Schwartz, A.: Die Definition des Geldes: Nettovermögen und Neutralität als Kriterien ..., p. 83

[29] See Streissler, E.W.: Endogenität und Neutralität des Geldes in theoriegeschichtlicher Perspektive, in: Schefold, B. (ed. by): Exogenität und Endogenität. Die Geldmenge in der Geschichte des ökonomischen Denkens und in der modernen Politik, Marburg 2002, pp. 65 - 88

[30] See Streissler, E.W.: Endogenität und Neutralität des Geldes ..., p. 67

ty)".[31] He also talks of economic absurdities as exogeneity and money neutrality.[32] Rejection of neutrality is hardly to be formulated more clearly. Streissler has attempted to contradict all arguments and proofs in his contribution to money neutrality from Hume over Archibald/Lipsey and Lucas to Samuelsen.[33] He concludes that monetary policy is difficult because it "nicht neutral sein kann (cannot be neutral)".[34]

2.2 Importance of Money Neutrality

Discussions on money neutrality clarify arguments and evidence for money neutrality originating on certain assumptions respectively conditions reflecting the viewpoint of the author.[35] It so happens that there are different viewpoints, approaches respectively views in the real world. Evaluation criteria must be available to evaluate success or flop of a theory. Therefore, questions arise concerning objectives of money respectively monetary policy to be achieved at the end. Assumed is guaranteeing money - respectively currency security, achieved by all theoreticians and practitioners responsible for monetary policies.

Viewpoints of members of the Austrian School can hardly be comprehensible. However, it can be agreed that in practice there is neither neutral money nor neutral monetary policy available. Considering money based on the above defined money quantity, it can be determined that money amount, as a whole, is not neutral at all. The statement made by Friedman is valid: only central bank money and cash are neutral.[36] Rest of the components of money amount are not neutral.

Therefore, the following question arises on how the Austrian School as well as all other deniers of money neutrality, guarantees money - respectively currency security? This particular aspect of monetary policies seems to be one of real significance. It is not only just money security issue (currency) under discussion but also protection of total economic systems facing internal (systemic) crisis. Money neutrality cannot be rejected on the basis of the up to now unsuccessful achievement of neutrality in practice. Rejection of money neutrality means accepting and doing nothing against permanent internal systemic economic crisis of all kinds and strengths.

If consequences of internal systemic economic crisis of wealth-, labor- and other losses are known, rejecting money neutrality and neglecting money security

---

[31] Streissler, E.W.: Endogenität und Neutralität des Geldes ..., p. 65

[32] See Streissler, E.W.: Endogenität und Neutralität des Geldes ..., p. 65

[33] See Streissler, E.W.: Endogenität und Neutralität des Geldes ..., pp. 74 - 84

[34] Streissler, E.W.: Endogenität und Neutralität des Geldes ..., p. 86

[35] See the discussion i.e. Koopmans, J.G.: Zum Problem des „Neutralen" Geldes, in: Hayek, F.A. (Ed.): Beiträge zur Geldtheorie, Wien 1933 (reprint Berlin a.o. 2007, pp. 211 – 359)

[36] See Friedman, M./Schwartz, A.: Die Definition des Geldes: Nettovermögen und Neutralität als Kriterien ..., p. 83

measures (of the currency) is a violation to the dignity of human rights. People, as we know have to be – according too many constitutions (German Constitution) – untouchable and protected.[37] Freedom and security are stipulated for citizens' elsewhere.[38]

The state has to materialize these judicially determined rights and thus money security (the currency). Appropriate strategies and measures are to be developed by monetary theories and -policies. Finally, politicians are responsible for its implementation. Prerequisites for creating neutral central bank money and neutral bank deposits are achievements of macro-economic equilibria. Consequently, there is no more saving possible. Except for cash, central bank money and neutral bank deposits are neutral at this specific situation. Furthermore, systemic economic crisis are avoided.

3. Counterfeit Protection

Third condition achieving money security is counterfeit protection. This condition is obvious. The more forged money on monetary markets, the more undermining influences on monetary policies of central banks. Central banks lose control possibilities on monetary policies and economic processes.

Guaranteeing counterfeit protection has always been a technical issue. Economic sectors can only contribute to solutions of counterfeit protection indirectly in creating economic environments. In creating economic environments money forgery becomes useless. Assumed is motivation forging money cannot be totally removed by creating affluence for all people – but at least it can be decreased. Jurisprudence can support this economic strategy. Money forgery could be even made less attractive in affluent societies by determining dissuasive measures.

Responsible money institutions actually have always been emphasizing difficulties of forging euros because of high security standards. However, vulnerable five- and ten euro bank notes have been substituted by new, forgery-proof bank notes.

Nevertheless, the well-known statement is also valid - here relating to security - one hundred percent (absolute) security is impossible. Security can only be relatively high and must be adjusted constantly to technical progress.

Consequently, it must be concluded, that in considering activities of individual citizens to money forgery, it can never be calculated at a hundred percent. A macro-economic equilibrium can only be reached approximately. Thus, a non-crisis economy can only be possible when all citizens comply with the laws.

---

[37] See i.e. Grundgesetz für die Bundesrepublik Deutschland in der im Bundesgesetzblatt Teil III, Gliederungspunkt 100-1, veröffentlichten Fassung, das zuletzt durch Artikel 1 des Gesetzes vom 11. Juli 2012 (BGBL. I p.1478) geändert worden ist, Art. 1

[38] See Konvention zum Schutz der Menschenrechte und Grundfreiheiten, vom 4. November 1950 (BGBl. 1952 p. 686), Art. 5

3.1 Technical Counterfeit Protection

One component of counterfeit protection of a currency is technical protection. Banknote- and coin units of a currency must be protected by technical features. A second option would be to manufacture the banknote- and coin units in a production process, impossible to be reproduced by unauthorized persons.

However, practice has been teaching us that both approaches guaranteeing counterfeit protection are not functioning properly. Every individual production process and every protection feature – conceived by people – can be copied by others. One can compare the guaranteed counterfeit of a currency protection to a competition between rabbit and hedgehog. Thus any technical edge of counterfeit currency protection can be easily reproduced by other people. It is just a question of time on how long it will take overtaking the edge by the opponents (counterfeiters).

Counterfeiting incentives depend largely - among other aspects - from currency significance. The higher the currency importance, the higher is the forgery incentive. Since the euro has been ranked as the second most important currency, counterfeiting incentives are accordingly high. The European Central Bank considers damages caused in the period between 2009 and 2010 at the minimum of 500 Mio. euro. Counterfeited discovered and secured money supplies have been increased by 11.6 percent, compared to the prior months during the second half of 2012. The European Central Bank anticipates still more increasing forged money quantities in the future. The number of yearly discovered illegal money-printing companies and mint establishments have led to this conclusion. The European Commission has drafted a proposal of a regulation towards the criminal protection of the euro and other currencies.[39]

3.2 Contribution of Economy to Counterfeit Protection

The topic whether the economy sector should contribute to counterfeit protection is important to be discussed. Economy contribution is creating a distribution of income and financial assets, assuring each individual person an appropriate income, so that currency forgery and other felonies would lose their interest.

This particular distribution would still have to be intensively discussed. Assumed is developing a new distribution theory.[40] It is known that the - thus far - contribution theories have not been able to establish themselves.

[39] See Europäische Kommission: Vorschlag für eine Richtlinie des Europäischen Parlaments und des Rates zum strafrechtlichen Schutz des Euro und anderer Währungen gegen Geldfälschung und zur Ersetzung des Rahmenbeschlusses 2000/383/JI des Rates, COM(2013) 42 final vom 2.5.2013 (2013/0023 (COD)), here p. 2

[40] See discussion on distribution theory i.e. Krelle, W.: Verteilungstheorie, Wiesbaden 1962; Pullen, J.: The marginal productivity theory of distribution: a critical history, London 2010

Consequently, the following conclusion can be derived – these theories have not as yet been able to offer convincing and acceptable solutions to the distribution issue. The publication of the Brundtland-Report has propagated sustainability approaches – approaches in finding new distribution theories by the United Nations. Next to social and ecological sustainability economical sustainability has been required. Economical sustainability is to be understood as the compensation between "poor" and "rich".[41] This compensation can only be assured by appropriate distributions. Basis for this has been formulated by a new distribution theory.[42]

4. Evaluation of Euro

Security evaluation of the euro can only be done, relatively in this particular framework, in comparison to the former German currency, the „deutschmark". An evaluation of the absolute security is empirically complicated (see below). Assessment of relative security of the euro should be emphasized because the euro is to be assessed by the perspective of the citizens. They compare the new currency – the euro – with the former currency – the „deutschmark".

New currency stability has generally been ranked worse than former currency. One can be aware of a certain habit. Since positive experiences have been made with former currency stability, belief in them remains strong. The euro, also known as "teuro"- as well as financial- and currency-issues in other euro-member-states, boost this specific judgment.

Principally, currency neutrality do not play specific roles in general discussions on new currency security. Currency security respectively money is rather a discussion aspect for the textbooks.

New currency counterfeit protection has been propagated at a considerable higher level by responsible institutions than counterfeit protection of former currencies. However, practice demonstrates continuous forgeries in euro-coins and euro-bank notes and it also demonstrates that new euro-bank notes (i.e. the five- and ten-euro bank notes) had to be developed.

---

[41] See Hauff, V. (Ed.): Unsere gemeinsame Zukunft. Der Brundtland-Bericht, Greven 1987, pp. XI, XV f., XXII, 1 f., 41 – 45, 46 - 69

[42] See previous work for a new distribution theory Witte, H.: Die nachhaltige Marktwirtschaft …

Tab. 3: Comparison between dm and euro regarding stability, neutrality, and counterfeit protection (intuitive values according to verbal estimations of currency in literature)[43]

comparison criterion	dm	Euro
stability	0.9	0.8
neutrality	0.1	0.1
forgery protection	0.9	0.9
security = (1+2+3)/3	0.63333	0.6

Source: own presentation evaluation scale: 0 to 1

It can be observed, German population has been quite skeptical regarding the new currency against the former currency, the „deutschmark". The intuitive evaluation only results in a small difference in security evaluation of the former and the new currency (compare tab. 3). A very important aspect of currency security, neutrality has unfortunately not sufficiently been discussed, whereas technical counterfeit protection has been estimated at a higher level by the official site. Support of technical counterfeit protection by the economy sector has not been pursued and thus it cannot be estimated. Changes caused by introducing the euro in the monetary system and the monetary theory are to be discussed in Part IV.

[43] For values calculated on basis of official statistics see part 7.

Part 4: Changes in Monetary System by Introducing Euro

Usually the euro has been compared with the "deutschmark" (dm). The "deutschmark" has been a relatively stable currency. Many citizens have been missing this particular feature with the euro. The situation before the introduction of the euro and the situation after the introduction must be explained to be able to express an opinion on the security of the euro. Comparison must be carried out on two levels. First, on levels of monetary- and currency theories and second, on levels of monetary- and currency policies. Possible changes should be explained and their impacts on euro security in comparison to the "deutschmark" identified. In a first step, monetary- and currency theories are examined for changes. Next changes in monetary- and currency policies are to be explained.

1. Changes in Money Amount Control Theories

Basis of monetary- and currency theories during the times of the "deutschmark" has been money amount controls supplemented by the Keynesian type. Regarding this, there have not been any specific alterations noted. Formulated differently, the euro introduction has not been based on alterations of theoretical basis. It should not be excluded that there have been and are currently published and discussed new contributions to money or rather money amount controls and to the interest rate theory in literature.

Changes of theoretical basis on the security of the euro in practical implementations have thus far not been perceived.

2. Changes in Practical Implementation of Monetary Policies

In practice, considerable changes in monetary- and currency policies have been caused by the euro introduction as compared to former times of the "deutschmark".

The most important change is that the Federal Republic of Germany respectively the Deutsche Bundesbank (German Federal Bank), is not the only one to determine monetary- and currency policies. In former times, the Bundesbank was authorized independently to decide on the application of instruments in monetary- and currency policies, guaranteeing the security of the "deutschmark". Principally, the Deutsche Bundesbank had only one further authority to comply with. It had to support policies of the Federal Republic of Germany in its monetary- and currency policy decisions. The Deutsche Bundesbank was able to implement the appropriate monetary- and currency policies.

The Deutsche Bundesbank is managed and administered by a management board (§ 7 BbankG). The management board of the Deutsche Bundesbank consists of the president, vice-president, and four additional members. Decisions are determined by the principle of a simple majority. The vote of the chairman decides in case of a tie. Either the president or the vice president leads the chair. Additionally to the board, the Deutsche Bundesbank is made up of nine headquarters (§ 8 BbankG), individually controlled by one president (the president of the headquarters), subject to the executive board of the Bundesbank. The headquarters have been founded in the section of one or more Federal States. The executive board of the Bundesbank transfers responsibilities to the individual headquarters (compare fig. 11).[1]

This particular situation has changed step by step, but fundamentally since the founding of the European Monetary Union, European System of Central Banks (ESCB) and implementation of the euro. The Deutsche Bundesbank is an integral component of the European System of Central Banks (§ 3 BbankG). Consequently it acts for central responsibility, guaranteeing price stability in the framework of the European System of Central Banks and is no longer authorized to decide alone. The Deutsche Bundesbank must decide with central banks of the other member states of the European Union to guarantee euro security by supporting decisions of monetary- and currency policies. However, central banks of other member states again must support policies of their own governments. At last, should decisions of central banks be considered, they should find support by the European Union.

Principally, there have not been any serious changes taking place, since introduction of the euro on monetary- and currency policies, because it is appropriate to structures and responsibilities of national central bank systems.

Major differences of the European System of Central Banks comparing former national central bank systems, is the coordination requirement. Coordination of monetary- and currency policies in the European System of Central Banks has become even more complicated than former national monetary- and currency policies with policies of national governments. Complexity results on one hand from increased numbers of decision makers and on the other hand, from different interest situations of decision makers. Different interest situations should actually not exist in the frame of an integration community. Since harmonization- and integration processes have not been finished yet in the European Union, there are currently still different interest situations complicating a coordination of monetary- and currency policies in the European System of Central Banks.

Increasing numbers of decision makers have been complicating coordination processes. Thus, it is known that the "unanimity rule" authorizes each individual member state a right to veto to prevent disadvantages resulting from a voting result already for a relatively small number of people with voting rights not being authorized any longer. Consequence is applying democratic majority rules and

---

[1] See Gesetz über die Deutsche Bundesbank (BbankG) vom 26.7.1957 in der Fassung vom 22.10.1992 (BGBL. I p. 1782)

acceptance of disadvantages with appropriate consequences, such as loss of motivation, etc. This particular issue can also not be solved by an exchange of votes for different other votes.

Complexity of vote of monetary- and currency political decisions is currently even greater because not all member states have introduced the euro yet. For that particular reason a transitional basis of still two monetary- and currency political systems of the European Systems in the European Union in which their interest situation must be coordinated.

On one hand, there is the European System of Central Banks (ESCB) and 28 central banks of the member states. On the other hand, the euro system exists consisting of 19 central banks of member states having already introduced the euro as the official currency. This is known as the European Monetary Union or rather the "Euro-19" (compare fig. 11).

Monetary- and currency policies of the European Union have been run by the European Central Bank and national central banks of member states having introduced the euro. Currency policies of member states having - thus far - not introduced the euro, responsibility remains unchanged with individual national central banks.[2]

The European System of the Central Banks (ESCB) is managed by the European Central Bank (ECB). The decision-making bodies of the European Central Bank (ECB) are the Board of Directors, and the ECB-Council.[3] The Board consists of the President, Vice-President, and four additional members. Current transactions of the European Central Bank (ECB) are managed by the Board of Directors.[4]

The ECB-Council consists of six members of the Board of Directors of the European Central Bank and presidents of national central banks of member states having already introduced the euro. Every individual member of the ECB-Council has one vote. However, when the number of members in the ECB-Council exceeds the limit of 21, there will be a distribution and a rotation of voting rights. Every member of the Board of Directors of the European Central Bank (ECB) has continuously one vote. Number of presidents eligible to vote is limited to 15.[5] Thus, there are a total of 21 votes in the ECB-Council. By limit-

---

[2] See Vertrag zur Gründung der Europäischen Gemeinschaft, Art. 282

[3] See Vertrag zur Gründung der Europäischen Gemeinschaft, Protokoll (Nr. 4), Über die Satzung des Europäischen Systems der Zentralbanken und der Europäischen Zentralbank, ABl. EU, C 83/230 from 30.3.2010, Art. 9; see for organization structure of the European Central Bank also i.e. Moritz, K.-H.: Geldtheorie und Geldpolitik, 3rd ed., München2012, p. 299 - 311

[4] See Vertrag zur Gründung der Europäischen Gemeinschaft, Protokoll (No. 4), Über die Satzung des Europäischen Systems der Zentralbanken und der Europäischen Zentralbank, ABl. EU, C 83/230 from 30.3.2010, Art. 11

[5] See Vertrag zur Gründung der Europäischen Gemeinschaft, Protokoll (No. 4), Über die Satzung des Europäischen Systems der Zentralbanken und der Europäischen Zentralbank, ABl. EU, C 83/230 from 30.3.2010, Art. 10

ing votes of presidents of national central banks to 15, the vote of the proportion of votes between Directorate of the European Central Bank and presidents of national central banks with increasing numbers of member states introducing the euro stay constant.

That actually means that each member – and thus also the presidents of national banks have now a 1/21 influence on monetary- and currency policies of central banks respectively of the euro system. Should the number increase over 21 persons, influence of the individual presidents of national central banks decreases because they have been formed with different numbers of votes?

Tab. 4: Distribution of votes in the ECB-Council at the 1st developing stage

group	votes of the groups	number of persons
presidents at the nat. CB	15	15
directorate ECB	6	6
total	21	21

Source: own presentation according to the Vertrag zur Gründung der Europäischen Gemeinschaft, Protokoll (No. 4), Über die Satzung des Europäischen Systems der Zentralbanken und der Europäischen Zentralbank, ABl. EU, C 83/230 from 30.3.2010, Art. 10

Three developing stages are needed to distinguish the euro. The proportion of votes has already been described and is demonstrated again in table 4.

If there are more than 15 member states introducing the euro, the second stage begins. There are now more than 21 persons in the ECB-Council. In addition to six members of the Directorate of the European Central Bank (ECB), there are 16 more presidents of national central banks. The third developing stage has been determined with 22 member states introducing the euro. The ECB-Council is then made up of more than 22 members. In addition to six members of the Directorate of the European Central Bank (ECB), there are 22 or more presidents of national central banks in the ECB-Council. In the second developing stage presidents of national central banks are classified into two groups and in the third developing stage in three groups (compare Tab. 5).

Tab. 5: Developing stages of the ECB-Council

developing stage	number of members in the ECB-Council from Directorate ECB	 nat. central banks	 sum	number of groups for presidents of the nat. CB
1	6	15	21	1
2	6	16 to 21	22 to 28	2
3	6	22 + x	28 + x	3

Source: own presentation according to the Vertrag zur Gründung der Europäischen Gemeinschaft, Protokoll (No. 4), Über die Satzung des Europäischen Systems der Zentralbanken und der Europäischen Zentralbank, ABl. EU, C 83/230 from 30.3.2010, Art. 10

In the second developing stage the first group includes five presidents of national central banks. Four votes have been allocated to the first group. However, only 11 votes have been allowed for the second group. The number of presidents of national central banks - between 11 and 16 - depends on individual numbers of member states having introduced the euro. Independent from the number of presidents of national central banks, there is a total of 15 votes; and the Directorate of the European Central Bank (ECB) has six. Thus, there is a total of 21 votes in the ECB-Council. The proportion between presidents of national central banks and the Directorate of the European Central Bank (ECB) has stayed constant in the opposite developing stage at 15 to 6 (compare Tab. 4 and 6).

Tab. 6: Contribution of votes in the ECB-Council according to groups in the 2nd developing stage

Groups	number of group members	votes of the group
1st president group	5	4
2nd president group	11 to 16	11
um 1st + 2nd	16 to 21	15
directorate ECB	6	6
sum votes total	-	21

Source: own presentation according to the Vertrag zur Gründung der Europäischen Gemeinschaft, Protokoll (No. 4), Über die Satzung des Europäischen Systems der Zentralbanken und der Europäischen Zentralbank, ABl. EU, C 83/230 from 30.3.2010, Art. 10

The third developing stage begins by introducing the euro in 22 or more member states. Presidents of national central banks are allocated into three groups. Furthermore, there are five presidents of national central banks in the first group. Additionally, the first group still has four votes. Half of the presidents of national central banks are in the second group (16 or more, it is rounded up with an odd number). Now the second group has only eight votes. The rest of the presidents of national central banks are located in Group 3 (6 or more). Group 3 has only three votes. However, the presidents of national central banks have still 15 votes, so that the proportion of votes between the Directorate of the European Central Bank has not been changed (compare Tab. 4, 6, and 7).

Since there are fewer votes in the three groups than presidents of national central banks, the right to vote changes, according to the rotation principle between the presidents of national central banks. Presidents of national central banks exert the right to vote for equal periods of time.

Allocation of member states respectively of their central banks to groups 1 to 3 is achieved, according to both criteria (1) proportion of aggregated gross national product to market prices and (2) proportion of total aggregated balance of money finance institutions. The first criterion has a 5/6 weight in calculating and the second one 1/6.

Tab. 7: Distribution of votes in the ECB-Council according to groups in the 3rd developing stage

groups	number of group members	votes of the group
1st presidential group	5	4
2nd presidential group	16 + x	8
3rd presidential group	6 + x	3
sum 1st to 3rd	22 + x	15
directorate ECB	6	6
sum of votes total	-	21

Source: own presentation according to the Vertrag zur Gründung der Europäischen Gemeinschaft, Protokoll (No. 4), Über die Satzung des Europäischen Systems der Zentralbanken und der Europäischen Zentralbank, ABl. EU, C 83/230 from 30.3.2010, Art. 10

Influence of national central banks of member states having introduced the euro results, not only from the above presented regulations of the European Union respectively European Monetary Union, but also from the practiced voting rule. Principally, the ECB-Council decides according to simple majority rule. In case of a tie, the vote of the President of the European Central Bank (ECB) is crucial. It shows, influence of individual member states can be located practically and clearly under the mentioned 1/21. Regarding capital of the ECB, transfer of currency reserves etc. (compare Ar. 28 - 33 of the Treaty establishing the European Community, Protocol (No. 4) and measures regulating organizations and decisions of the ECB-Council, other voting regulations are to applied to – discussing these connections now is not necessary.

Additionally to the ECB-Council, there is the Extended ECB-Council as the third decision-making body of the European Central Bank (ECB) (compare fig. 11). In the Extended ECB-Council, president and vice-president, as well as presidents of national central banks of member states of the European Union. Additional members of the Directorate may not participate without the right to vote at meetings of the Extended ECB-Council. The Extended ECB-Council is, above all, responsible for such tasks, resulting from exceptions for one or more member states, after the euro introduction has been achieved.[6]

Fig. 11: Changes in practical implementation of monetary policy (money amount- and interest control)

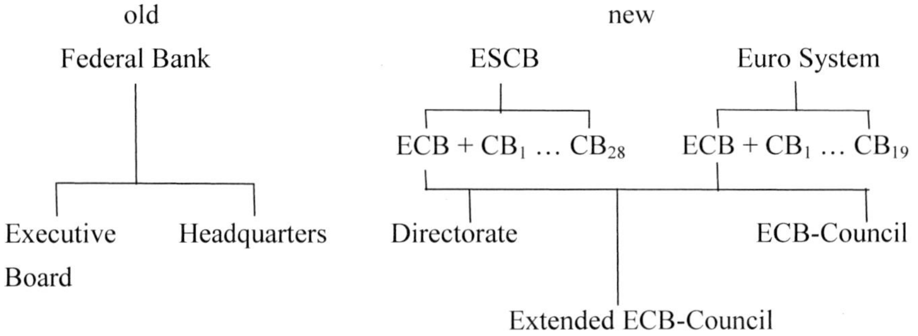

Source: own presentation according to Article 282 Vertrag über die Arbeitsweise der Europäischen Union; Bundesbank-Gesetz, especially §7 and 8

Fig. 11 emphasizes that monetary- and currency policy decisions have required substantially more demands in coordinating the creation of the European System of Central Banks (ESCB), compared to situations at the time of the „deutschmark". From a German perspective the Deutsche Bundesbank has had the decision-making power formerly. Today, there are more decision-makers taking part in the euro system. Decision-making has risen accordingly. Today 19 respectively 28 central banks are participating in decision-making processes of monetary- and currency policies.

National governments of member states have been committed to serve their people and have not yet been able to reach a common interest situation, because harmonization- and integration processes have not been achieved yet.

---

[6] See Vertrag zur Gründung der Europäischen Gemeinschaft, Protokoll (No. 4), Über die Satzung des Europäischen Systems der Zentralbanken und der Europäischen Zentralbank, ABl. EU, C 83/230 from 30.3.2010, Art. 43 - 46

2.1 Many States with Different Economic Structures

Member states of the European Union are still demonstrating different economic structures because they have not yet been able to adopt any harmonizing- and integrating processes.[7] Such, as wages, taxes, prices, etc. have not yet been equalized. One could say that member states still have different interests. Consequently, there are different preferences emerging from these different interest situations. Naturally, these differences complicate votes regarding policy decisions. A unanimity rule has not been practicable in votes. Democratic majority rules can only be applied in compensations respectively compromises. Compensations respectively compromises principally complicate optimum decisions or make it even impossible. Especially in monetary- and currency policy votes, this fact can really be of a considerable disadvantage, because necessary money quantity- and interest objectives are not able to be achieved at a hundred percent.

2.2 Many Central Banks in European System of Central Banks

All national central banks of the European System of Central Banks must represent the interests of national member states or rather their governments. Votes of the European Central Bank are tangent to all these particular interest situations. All of these aspects arrive at the above described disadvantages.

3. Can Convergence Criteria Guarantee Functions and Security of Euro?

Solution of vote difficulties in the European System of Central Banks based on different national interest situations shall be reached with the support of convergence criteria. All member states of the European Union planning to introduce the euro have to comply with the determined Maastricht[8] 1992 convergence criteria.

The four convergence criteria listed:

(1) Price stability, that is, a member state must assure a sustainable price stability and an average inflation rate. It should not exceed the inflation rate, regarding the three best member states at not more than 1.5 %-points. In doing so the inflation rate is measured by the consumer price index with a comparable basis – however, under observance of different definitions in the individual member states.

---

[7] See for effects of EU-Enlargement i.e. Cohen, B.J.: Enlargement and the International Role of the Euro, in: Review of International Political Economy, Vol. 14 (2007), pp. 746 – 773

[8] See Vertrag über die Europäische Union (Maastricht-Vertrag) vom 7. Februar 1992 (ABl. EG Nr. C 224 v. 31.8.87. 1992), 6. Protokoll über die Konvergenzkriterien nach Artikel 109j des Vertrages zur Gründung der Europäischen Gemeinschaft, esp. Art. 1 – 4

(2) Financial situation of public authorities – a council decision, according to Article 104c paragraph 6 of the contract is not available for concerned member states with excessive deficits. However, up to 3% of the gross domestic product is not seen as a deficit and a government debt up to 60 % of gross domestic products.[9]

(3) Participation at the Exchange Rate Mechanism of the European Monetary System, this means a member state has to comply within the frame of the rate mechanism intended normal bandwidths (± 15 %). Member states are not allowed to have devalued their central parities of their currencies against currencies of any other member states during the last two years before having changed to the euro.

(4) Convergence of interest rates, this means that one year before the euro introduction the average long lasting nominal interest rate in a member state may not be set at more than two percentage points above the appropriate value not exceeding the three best member states regarding the price stability, exhibiting the best results. In this procedure the interest rates are measured by long termed government bonds or comparable securities in compliance with the different definitions in the individual member states (Dublin 1996) have been corrected (s.b.).

It is especially important to examine whether compliance with the convergence criteria has taken place before the introduction of the euro has to be created or rather has been created.

The idea determining convergence criteria at the time of introduction of the euro is the harmonization of the monetary- and currency political framework conditions in the member states in introducing the euro as currency.

Price stability is the first criterion – a consequential application of the – perhaps - most important condition to secure the functions of a currency. The condition has already been represented in theory and practice before introducing the euro. Sense and success of this particular criterion have already been proven by the unanimously recognized security of the former "deutschmark". However, whether or not the successful application of the criterion could be concluded a success in a common currency, depends on conditions determined for the application of the particular criterion.

These conditions allow principally (see above) a deviation of 1.5 percentage points of the ideal value 'zero'. However, deviation from the ideal value is practically higher due to two reasons. The reference value for the allowed is just not the ideal value, but a (assumed distorted) mean value made up of the inflation rates of the three member states with the lowest inflation rate. Additionally, the

[9] See Vertrag über die Europäische Union (Maastricht-Vertrag) vom 7. Februar 1992 (ABl. EG Nr. C 224 v. 31.8.87. 1992), 6. Protokoll über die Konvergenzkriterien nach Artikel 109j des Vertrages zur Gründung der Europäischen Gemeinschaft, esp. Art. 1 – 4

calculation of the inflation rate of the national differences regarding the definition of the consumer price index is being considered. By calculating the allowed deviations from the ideal value, it is impossible to calculate precisely the difference to the ideal value. Thus, it can be concluded, that the criterion "price stability" in the common currency euro does not guarantee the same good results regarding the security of the currency – such as i.e. the national currency "deutschmark" has done before.

The second convergence criterion is, in regard to the criterion of the government budgetary – it is not allowed to be marked by a considerable deficit. This particular criterion should guarantee the security of the currency to prevent a high deficit and/or a high indebtedness of a member state. Percentage values for the deficit and the national indebtedness on the gross domestic product have been determined.

Objective of this particular convergence criterion is reasonable and important. However, whether or not a limitation on the deficit and the national indebtedness is effective can hardly be assessed on theoretical basis of different assumptions on different theories. Practical experiences with constantly increasing and inability to dampen the national debt in many nations globally, have created doubts in the limitation of this particular issue. It is also the theoretical knowledge speaking against its effectiveness.[10] Short-termed effects on the limitation of the deficit and national debt before the introduction of the euro – however, cannot be totally excluded.

The third convergence criterion – participation on the currency exchange mechanism of the European Monetary System – requires the compliance of the normal bandwidth of the national currency against the currency of a member state within the last two years before the introduction of the euro has taken place. A diverging trend in monetary- and currency policy sectors is actually avoided – however, it does not affect harmonization at all.

The fourth convergence criterion – the convergence of the interest rates - requires the adjustment of interest rates. The long-term nominal rate is allowed to be two percentage points above the reference value. The nominal interest rate value of three member states with the lowest inflation or rather the highest price stability is valid for the reference value. However, a deviation of this particular ideal value should be just above two percentage points, because in estimating the interest rates of long-termed government bonds or comparable, securities are to be assumed. Different national definitions are considered by determination, so that deviations above two percentage points of the ideal value cannot surely be avoided.

Concluding the assessment of the convergence criteria, regarding effectiveness of guarantees of functions of the euro and its security is fully effective on the

[10] See Witte, H.: Die nachhaltige Marktwirtschaft, pp. 55 – 68, esp. p. 62 - 68

basis of allowed deviations of ideal values, not necessarily given. Thus an estimation can only be given under the reference of an objective or rather reference model. Effectiveness of convergence criteria should be clarified by an example.

Assumed is just a deviation of 1.5 or rather 2 percentage points in the trajectory of a flight to the moon in a rocket or rather spacecraft – added – an additional not exactly calculable difference of x percentage points - cannot be calculated. Then, the question arises who would respond in booking such a flight to the moon? However, the monetary- and currency policies have already been booked before these particular conditions - before introducing the euro.

Convergence criteria refer just to the monetary- and currency policy aspects. Structural differences in individual member states without influence on economic processes and monetary- and currency policies are not tangent to the criteria. Differences are consequently not - respectively have not been harmonized yet.

Convergence criteria just refer to the time of introduction of the euro by a member state. For issues occurring after stability- and growth pacts have been created, will be discussed in the following.

4. Can Stability- and Growth Pact Guarantee Functions and Security?

In the Stability- and Growth Pact[11] (preparation at the meetings of the European, Council of the Heads of State and Government in Dublin 1996 and Noordwijk 1997; Resolution Amsterdam 1997) determined to be complied by all member states of the euro system at the time after the euro introduction to promote stability and growth.

Conditions are:

(1) Maximum yearly new indebtedness of states of 3 percent of gross domestic products.

(2) Maximum total indebtedness of public budgets of 60% of gross domestic products.

(3) By neglecting these particular values, finance ministers of other member states are eligible to determine sanctions.

These conditions are appropriate to the convergence criteria 2. A second estimation is therefore unnecessary. It can be referred to above mentioned presentations to convergence criteria. Merely condition 3 is the new one. Condition 3 can be seen as an aggravation of the situation of member states not having classified its national finances according to the rules.

This is presented with four possible sanctions. According to this a member:

---

[11] See Entschließung des Rates vom 17. Juni 1997 über den Stabilitäts- und Wachstumspakt, ABl. EG Nr. C 236 vom 2. August 1997, p. 1

(1) State can be imposed with the following punishments for having an excessive deficit: a fine of 0.2 to 0.5 percent of its gross domestic product; (2) with obligation to deposit of non-interest bearing deposits at an adequate level.

(3) With announcements of additional particulars before bonds, as well as other securities having occurred and (4) with a related change of the lending policy of the European Investment Bank.

5. Change of Stability- and Growth Pact by Six-Pack

Stability- and growth pact has been reformed by the Six-Pack,[12] stability- of a Six-Pack because the reform has been established into six regulations respectively guidelines. Three regulations and one guideline refer to budget policy and two on macro-economic disequilibria. The Six-Pack was set into force on December 13, 2011. Determined were the standard values for yearly public deficits (3% of gross domestic product) and debt repayment status (60% of gross domestic products). Member states with higher debt repayment statuses are ordered to reduce their debt repayment status – also – in such cases when yearly public deficits are below 3% of gross domestic products.

For member states of the European Monetary System, deficit procedures have been pending, or not becoming active in case of an early warning of the ECONFIN-COUNCIL, an interest bearing deposit of 0.1% of gross domestic products can be determined. ECONFIN-Council can activate interest-bearing deposits to determine in the amount of 0.1% of gross domestic products. In further non-compliance of the reference value or rather non-observance of the recommendations of the ECONFIN-Council, the deposit can at first, change into a non-interest bearing deposit and then into a fine.

[12] See Six-Pack consisting of (1) Verordnung (EU) No. 1175/2011 des Europäischen Parlaments und des Rates vom 16. November 2011 zur Änderung der Verordnung (EG) No. 1466/97 des Rates über den Ausbau der haushaltspolitischen Überwachung und der Überwachung und Koordinierung der Wirtschaftspolitiken, ABl. EU L 306/12, 23.11.2011, (2) Verordnung (EU) No. 1177/2011 des Rates vom 8. November 2011 zur Änderung der Verordnung (EG) No. 1467/97 über die Beschleunigung und Klärung des Verfahrens bei einem übermäßigem Defizit, ABl. EU L 306/33, 23.11.2011, (3) Verordnung (EU) No. 1173/2011 des Europäischen Parlaments und des Rates vom 16. November 2011 über die wirksame Durchsetzung der haushaltspolitischen Überwachung im Euro-Währungsgebiet, ABl. EU L 306/1, 23.11.2011, (4) Richtlinie 2011/85/EU des Rates vom 8. November 2011 über die Anforderungen an die haushaltspolitischen Rahmen der Mitgliedstaaten, ABl. EU L 306/41, 23.11.2011, (5) Verordnung (EU) No. 1176/2011 des Europäischen Parlaments und des Rates vom 16. November 2011 über die Vermeidung und Korrektur makroökonomischer Ungleichgewichte, ABl. EU L 306/25, (6) Verordnung (EU) No. 1174/2011 des Europäischen Parlaments und des Rates vom 8. November 2011 über Durchsetzungsmaßnahmen zur Korrektur übermäßiger makroökonomischer Ungleichgewichte im Euro-Währungsgebiet, ABl. EU L 306/8, 23.11.2011

Additionally, the voting procedure has been changed by the council. Thus, a deficit procedure can now be quicker introduced. Furthermore, the national accounts, statistics, and forecast procedures of member states have been adjusted to the EU-Standard. Member states reporting false data can be punished with additional fines.

An early warning system for macro-economic disequilibria and appropriate correction procedures have been determined in the judicial measures five and six. The early warning system consists of indicators to foreign- and private debts as well as to competitiveness.

The tightening stability- and growth pact, actually exerting conditions on budgetary discipline in the Euro-States by 'Six-Pack' could not solve issues. Early allowed divergence of 3 percent equilibrium and long termed allowed divergence of 60 percent, emphasize just how far it is, reaching a national equilibrium. Necessary stringent economies achieving budgetary discipline will show negative effects and will not lead to an equilibrium. For that particular purpose an equilibrium in the economies would have to be carried out. It is also hardly possible to apply the early warning system successfully. It is well-known in other sectors that the early warning systems cannot be without criticism or failure in practice.[13]

6. No Equilibria and Missing Harmonization

Criticism on convergence criteria and on stability- and growth pact or rather the Six-Pack is that by this, there is – first, no assurance in equilibria of member states of the euro system and second, no harmonization of economic structures and economic conditions achieved. Both are to be seen as important prerequisites for avoiding economic crisis.

Creation of (market-) equilibria is a very old requirement of the economy – as it has already been stated by Adam Smith.[14] It is amazing on how the requirement has hardly found any consideration or rather not at all – in economic practice. This fact is even more amazing, because it is just logical, that there are no crisises occurring in case of equilibria. Every individual person lives, according to this principle. The human body is at the state of equilibrium. Medical doctors say an individual is healthy. Whenever the body equilibrium deviates – the result means illness. An illness, that has to be treated to get the individual back into an equilibrium state.

---

[13] See i.e. Moder, M.: Supply Frühwarnsysteme, Wiesbaden 2008, esp. pp. 195 ff., 241 ff.; Kryste, U.: Frühwarnsysteme, in: Hutzschenreuter, T./Griess-Nega, T. (Ed.): Krisenmanagement, Wiesbaden 2006, pp. 221 – 244; Schneider, W.: Früherkennung und Intuition, Wiesbaden 2011, esp. pp. 211 ff.

[14] See Smith, A.: Der Wohlstand …, pp. LVI f., 415, 507, 509

This particular knowledge could also be transferred to the economy sector. The fact that – even though – convergence criteria and stability- and growth-pack or rather Six-Pack have been applied – however economic crisis have still been occurring. This effect can be proven by the known crisis in Greece, Cypress, Spain, Italy, etc.[15]

7. Stability versus Growth

Objective of convergence criteria and of stability- and growth-pack respectively the Six-Pack is to ensure simultaneously, stability and growth of member states of the European Union. It is therefore necessary to examine whether stability and growth are two compatible objectives. These are the three following situations:

(1) a stable equilibrium,

(2) an instable equilibrium

and

(3) no equilibrium.

The first case represents stability. Growth would destroy stability – except - a balanced growth could be achieved. It would also be true for the second case - only balanced growth would maintain stability. Thus there would be at last a possibility – just – in the third case, creating an unstable equilibrium. In summary, growth cannot be seen as a general pharmaceutics to guarantee stability.

Creating growth should be examined as a second criterion. In this case there is reference to economic production functions, such as the Cobb-Douglas-Production-Function. This particular production function shows economic performance (x), created by both integration factors (complete production factors summarizing factors), labor (L) and capital (CA). It makes up the total economic achievement (x), which is set up by both integration factors (all production factors completed factors), labor (L) and capital (CA). Growth (x_2 - x_1) is created according to total economic production. Growth (x_2 - x_1) is created according to the total production function through the yearly increase of the total economic performance (x_2 - x_1) by increased performance (x_2 - x_1) by the increased input of labor (L_2 - L_1) and capital. This context is demonstrated in fig. 12. Since total economic performance – labor and capital – consists of three different units of measurement measured in different units of measurement, they can only be determined as index values in fig. 12 values without units of measurement.[16]

---

[15] See i.e. Wittmann, W.: Von der Finanzkrise zur Schuldenkrise, in: Review of Economics, Vol. 62 (2011), pp. 40 - 55

[16] See the explanations for this production function made by Cobb and Douglas: Cobb, C.W./ Douglas, P.H.: A Theory of Production, in: American Economic Review, Vol. XVIII (1928), Supplement, pp. 139 165, here p. 140

Noted from fig. 12 is the creation of a growth effect that brings about different combination possibilities of integration factors - labor and capital. Just three combination possibilities are presented here. The first possibility is presented on the y-axis. Just the production factor labor is necessary for creating growth. The integration factor capital is not implemented (CA = 0). Opposition factor is presented on the x-axis. Only the production factor capital is implemented for growth. The integration factor labor is not implemented for the creation of growth (L = 0). Combination possibility requiring the same input in a growth effect of labor and capital (L = CA), is represented by a 45-degree line.

It is essential to prove the combination relationship availability of work and capital. In the economy a growth effect shall be generated for the practical economic policy and assessment of its growth targets.

Well-known in practice less and less work has become available and more and more capital has to be introduced to create sophisticated production performance due to labor-saving and capital-intensive technical progress. Consequently, in a constant presence of growth in labor-saving and capital-intensive progress a decrease of labors can be observed in fig. 12. This process runs theoretically up to the point where growth is not creating any more labor any longer.

This situation has been reached when the combination possibility of labor and capital are represented by the x-axis. The input of the integration factor labor is zero.

However, it must remain open whether or not and at what time this particular situation has been reached in practice. However, clear is, that labor-saving and capital-intensive technical progress continuously create less and less new jobs by growth. Capital requirements have been increasing more and more.

Fig. 12: Impacts of growth

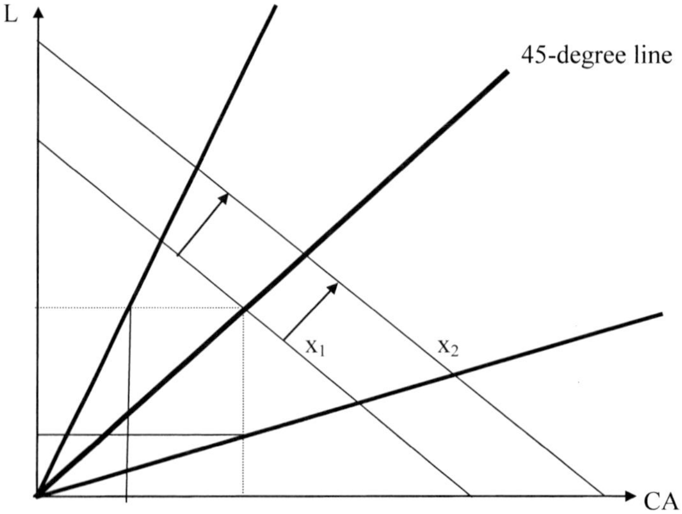

Source: own presentation

8. No Unlimited Growth

Summarizing fig. 12 it could be concluded that growth is going on indefinitely respectively presented growth effects could be extended indefinitely. An indefinite growth would require available indefinite amounts of integration factors. It just might be possible to extend the quantity of capital up to infinity. Factor 'labor' – however – can hardly be increased indefinitely because there is neither enough manpower nor machines – an appropriate amount of production factors, available. However, this is not the case. The number of production factors available on planet Earth is limited. This is described as scarce production factors (resources).

Thus, economic growth has been limited on planet Earth. The law of decreasing growth rates is valid. Growth rate (gr) approach asymptotically to a maximum value – called stagnation (compare fig. 13).

Fig. 13: Limited growth

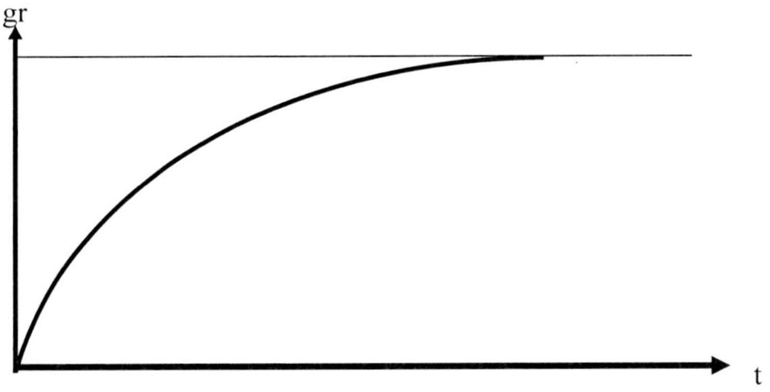

Source: own presentation

The presented growth process in fig. 13 is not only valid for the economy. Growth processes known from nature undergo the same process. After a beginning growth process development goes into the stagnation process. Every individual person can observe this growth process. At a beginning of growth processes, individuals continuously grow up to the point of stagnation. This growth process is also true with plants and animals.

Recognized is the growth rate (gr) gradually in time (t) decreasing. The law of decreasing growth rates is valid. Extended growth – not according to the law of growth by nature – means for animals, plants, and individual persons a morbid condition has occurred. This signifies crisis in the economy sector. Since produced quantities cannot be sold, maximum demand is inefficient. Thus - crisis occur.

9. Summary

To sum up, changes have not been based on the euro introduction on monetary-

and currency theories. Changes have only been occurring in the monetary- and currency system. Member states of the euro system are, regarding monetary- and currency policies, no longer independent. They must match monetary- and currency policy decisions with other member states of the euro system. Consequently, monetary- and currency policy decision mechanisms have become more and more complex and any individual member state of the euro system has had less influence on monetary- and currency policies than ever before.

New regulations have been created to meet the function of the euro system. They have to be complied with all member states of the euro system. The above discussed new regulations are supposed to secure stability and growth of currency areas. Stability is only reached by limited means through applying new regulations because it is impossible to create economic equilibria. Regulations must be supplemented by regulations to create economic equilibria. To what extent growth is necessary at all respectively is desired, requires an intensive discussion from an ecological and equilibrium theoretic viewpoint.[17]

[17] For other effects of the implementation of the euro see i.e. Bris, A./Koskinen, Y./Nilson, M.: The Euro and Corporate Valuations, in: The Review of Financial Studies, Vol. 22 (2009), pp. 3171 – 3209

Part 5: Alternative Suggestions to secure the Euro - not leading to an Equilibrium

A multitude of approaches has been developed for securing the euro. Selected proposals should be discussed and commented briefly. To begin with, there have already been recognized significant differences in the framework of approaches to be developed. Currently discussed approaches do not assume equilibrium solutions.

The following approaches are being discussed:

(1) rescue package (volume 500 Bill. euro),

(2) exit from of the euro system or rather the euro zone

- Greek´s exit
- exit taken by the Federal Republic of Germany (estimated costs 295 – 390 Bill. Euros),

(3) euro as a parallel currency

(4) euroization

(5) dual money union with a north- and a south currency as well as

(6) political union.

Alternative approaches clearly demonstrate on how far apart assumptions for a solution of the euro-issues are. No uniform opinion on how to get to an effective solution is possible.

1. Rescue package

Four sets of measures are understood for ensuring the euro under the Euro-Rescue- respectively protection shielding of the euro.

These sets of measures are:

- European Financial Stabilization Mechanism (EFSM)
- European Financial Stabilization Facility (EFSF)
- European Stabilization Mechanism (ESM)
- Fiscal Pact (the European Fiscal Union) and
- bilateral credits of the EU-Member States

The following discussion on these measure sets should be carried out. Appropriate literature should demonstrate a detailed presentation.[1]

1.1 European Financial Stabilization Mechanism (EFSM)

The European Financial Stabilization Mechanism (EFSM) is an instrument created by the European Union to help member states in financial difficulties. Thus, it is an EU-instrument. The instrument provides payment support of the European Commission to member states having financing costs, too high. This is the case, whenever one member state has a refinancing demand by a decrease of its bond courses and increasing rates of return in refinancing demands. The EU-Commission provides payment supports based on its very excellent rating to refinance clearly lower rates.

Volumes of the European Financial Stabilization Mechanism amount to 60 Bill. euros. The part of the Federal Republic of Germany is 20% respectively around 12 Bill. euro.

1.2 European Financial Stabilization Facility (EFSF)

The European Financial Stabilization Facility (EFSF)[2] should help states in crisis – members in the European Monetary Union (having introduced the euro). An application can be formulated by any member state of the EMU not being able to refinance itself with non-affordable high interests due to bad credit standings respectively bad ratings.

The European Financial Stability Facility (EFSF) consists of a system of credits and guarantees. Credit volume amounts to 440 Bill. euros. Guarantee volume amounts to 440 Bill. euros. Guaranteed volume is 780 Bill. euros. For the introduction of the credit- and guarantee currency, the European Union has founded a limited corporation (Ltd.), according to the Luxembourgian Rights, the Special Purpose Vehicle (SPV).

The European Financial Stabilization Facility has refinanced itself for credit distributions for more improved conditions than the crisis states. Thus, there is not any money flowing from one EU-Member State to another. The EU-States are

[1] See i.e. Schuppan, N.: Die Euro-Krise. Ursachen, Verlauf, makroökonomische und europarechtliche Aspekte und Lösungen, München 2014; Schachtschneider, K.A.: Euro-Rettungspolitik – unvernünftig, rechtlos und staatswidrig, in: Lachmann, W. (Ed.): Die Zukunft des Euros, Berlin 2012, pp. 90 – 215; Hunfeld, M.: ESM und Fiskalpakt: Staatsressourcenpolitik für die Europäische Union, in: Meyer, D. (Ed.): Die Zukunft der Währungsunion, Berlin 2012, pp. 135 – 156; Meyer, D.: Zur juristischen Begründung des „Rettungsschirms“: Eine ökonomische Plausibilitätskontrolle, in: Review of Economics, Vol. 61 (2010), pp. 103 - 124

[2] See Gesetz zur Übernahme von Gewährleistungen im Rahmen eines europäischen Stabilisierungsmechanismus (Stabilisierungsmechanismusgesetz – StabMechG) vom 22. Mai 2010 (BGBl. I, p. 627)

only liable. The amount guaranteed by the Federal Republic of Germany is 211 Bill. euros. Improved refinancing conditions for the European Refinancing Facility result from high rating values, determined by rating agencies based on acceptance of high rating values of the most important liable EU-Member States.

European Financial Stabilization Facility has next to instruments of credit- and guarantee-granting to crisis states, four additional instruments from the euro system: (1) financial precautionary support for euro system member states, having short termed financial problems – else, principally – with a solid basis of data, (2) preventive financial support to recapitalize financial institutions, that is financial institutions, that is, credits to EMU-States for the provision of recapitalization of financial institutions, (3) primary market purchasing, that is, purchases from newly issued government bonds on the primary market (market of issue), to keep the individual states on the market or enable them to return back to the market and (4) secondary market purchasing, that is, government bonds traded on the secondary market (circulation market) for the support of the bond markets respectively for the price management of government bonds of "crisis-ridden" states.

1.3 European Stability Mechanism (ESM)

European Stability Mechanism (ESM) is an according to international law, irredeemable contract of member states of the euro system.[3] The contract of setting up the European Stability Mechanism came into force on the September 27, 2012. In this way the European Finance Stability Mechanism and Finance Stability Facility (EFSF) were detached from the European Stability Mechanism. The share capital of thc European Stability Mechanism amounts to 700 Billion euros (see Chapter 3, Art. 8, and attachment II of the contract). There are 80 Bill. euros deposited and 620 Bill. euros withdrawal. The distribution of the liability risk and the financing is according to the capital components of the member states at the European Central Bank (ECB) (see Chapter 3, Art. 11, and attachment I of the contract). The European Stability Mechanism is distinguished from the European Finance Stability Mechanism and the European Finance Stability Facility (EFSF) by the deposit share. Both predecessors before the European Stability Mechanism (ESM) did not have any deposits. They have just taken out loans and passed them on to the state of crisis.

---

[3] See Bekanntmachung über das Inkrafttreten des Vertrags zur Einrichtung des Europäischen Stabilitätsmechanismus (ESM) vom 1. Oktober 2012 (BGBl. II, p.1086); Vertrag zur Errichtung des Europäischen Stabilitätsmechanismus zwischen dem Königreich Belgien, der Bundesrepublik Deutschland, der Republik Estland, Irland, der Hellenischen Republik, dem Königreich Spanien, der Französischen Republik, der Italienischen Republik, der Republik Zypern, dem Großherzogtum Luxemburg, Malta, dem Königreich der Niederlande, der Republik Österreich, der Portugiesischen Republik, der Republik Slowenien, der Slowakischen Republik und der Republik Finnland vom 2. Februar 2012 (BGBl. II, pp. 981, 983)

Objectives of the European Stability Mechanism (ESM) are described as the following:[4] (1) prevention of state insolvencies, (2) stabilization of national bonds, and decreasing of interests, (3) creation of longer extended periods to implement recovery programs of crisis states, (4) relief of European and globally spread bank sectors regarding governments bonds of crisis states, and (5) signalizing determination maintaining the European Monetary Union (EMU) and above all - the euro.

1.4 The European Fiscal Pact

The European Fiscal Pact, in other words, the contract of stability, coordination, and control in the Economic Monetary Union (EMU) set up on March 2, 2012,[5] supplements the European Stability Mechanism (1) introduction of national debt brake – budget deficit must not exceed 3.0% of gross domestic product, (2) public debts should not exceed 60% of gross domestic product to market prices or (3) in an appropriate form reducing to this particular value, (4) to enforce an economic- and fiscal reform- and adjustment programs and to have it controlled externally on a regular basis, as well as (5) accomplish or rather have a fundamental and intensive analysis of structural government debts executed.

1.5 Bilateral Credits of EU-Member States

Additionally to the instruments created by the European Union for distressed member states of the euro system, there are other instruments. These include bilateral credits, granted by other member states. These particulars breach the "non-solidarity clause"[6], according to the responsibility of each individual member state to operate and to be liable for its own debts.

---

[4] See i.e. Schuppan, N.: Die Euro-Krise ..., p. 155

[5] See Gesetz zu dem Vertrag vom 2. März 2012 über Stabilität, Koordinierung und Steuerung in der Wirtschafts- und Währungsunion vom 13. September 2012 (BGBl. II, p. 1006); Vertrag über Stabilität, Koordinierung und Steuerung in der Wirtschafts- und Währungsunion zwischen dem Königreich Belgien, der Republik Bulgarien, dem Königreich Dänemark, der Bundesrepublik Deutschland, der Republik Estland, Irland, der Hellenischen Republik, dem Königreich Spanien, der Französischen Republik, der Italienischen Republik, der Republik Zypern, der Republik Lettland, der Republik Litauen, dem Großherzogtum Luxemburg, Ungarn, Malta, dem Königreich der Niederlande, der Republik Österreich, der Republik Polen, der Portugiesischen Republik, Rumänien, der Republik Slowenien, der Slowakischen Republik, der Republik Finnland und dem Königreich Schweden, Titel III, Fiskalpolitischer Pakt vom 2. März 2012 (BGBl. II, p. 1008)

[6] See Vertrag über die Arbeitsweise der Europäischen Union (konsolidierte Fassung), ABl. EU C 326/47 vom 26.10.2012, Art. 125

1.6 Evaluating Set of Measures of Euro-Rescue Package

All presented approaches to support crisis affected member states of the euro system contribute indirectly to the security of the euro. There is no contribution to both criteria for money security, neutrality and counterfeit protection. Contribution to stability criterion is just indirect and short termed. States with financial difficulties based on a too high national debt situation are helped. By this procedure an indirect and short termed support for stabilizing the euro is being rendered. Causes and long-termed impacts of too high national debts – however – are not rectified or rather solved.

The European Union has thoroughly acknowledged the only short termed effect of relief operations and has created the European Fiscal Pact. Conditions for relief operations have been set up for badly affected member states to comply with. Long-termed structural changes and adjustment measures have been called for. However, economic equilibria cannot be successfully created by the prescribed measures. This, however, would be the only solution to guarantee the third criterion - stability - and therefore security for the euro. Furthermore, it would be important to check to what extent measures would support solving structural issues demonstrated by Piketty.[7]

This specified criticism has also been valid for embodied measures having been described as inactive instruments respectively measures for rescuing of badly affected member states. These are, euro bills, and debt repayment funds.[8]

2. Exit from Euro System

Principally, every member state is able to find its own solution to exit the euro system. Exiting the euro system is a decision every member state desiring to exit should be calculating possible advantages or disadvantages. If advantages outweigh disadvantages a member state will exit. However, exiting the euro system has just been a hypothetical discussion up to now. Discussion ignited on the topic of the crisis-situation „Greece“. Thus, discussion points have been the Greece exit as well as the German one.

---

[7] See Piketty, T.: Das Kapital im 21. Jahrhundert, München 2014

[8] See Sachverständigenrat zur Begutachtung der gesamtwirtschaftlichen Entwicklung: Der Europäische Schuldentilgungspakt – Fragen und Antworten, Arbeitspapier 01/2012, Stand: 25.Januar 2012, http://www.sachverständigenrat-wirtschaft.de (called upon 12.17.2014); EU-Kommission: Expertengruppe soll Schuldentilgungsfonds und prüfen, http://ec.europa.eu/deutschland/press/pr_releases/11527_de.htm. (called upon 10.22.2014)

2.1 Greek Exit

Since Greece, as first member state of the euro system has been getting into serious difficulties, experts have been discussing the Greece exit from the euro system (Grexit) as the solution of the issue.[9] Exit from the euro system can be applied by any other individual member state of the euro system. Greek exit from the euro system would actually mean that Greece would have to introduce its own currency. Administrative technical, legal, and political consequences should not be discussed at this point.[10]

The Greece exit from the euro system would suspend all responsibilities to monetary- and currency policies to Greece from all member states of the euro system. However, this assumed advantage – contradicts monetary- and currency policy objectives of the European Union. The extended responsibilities of the European Union toward support consists is to be examined. Greece will still be a member of the European Union – even though the exit from the euro system had taken place. The Greek exit would probably not have indirect effects on stability, neutrality, and counterfeit protection on the euro.

2.2 Federal Republic of Germany Exit

The Federal Republic of Germany exit has also been discussed,[11] as an alternative. This alternative has been ranked equally to the associated consequences, impacts, advantages, and disadvantages, just as the Greece exit issue has been done before. There is – however, a difference between a Greek- and a German exit from the euro system regarding individual economic power and associated capabilities to survive withdrawal and its consequences successfully.[12]

3. Euro - Parallel Currency

The parallel currency concept[13] for solving the euro-crisis has also been brought to discussion. Concept plans setting up a national currency parallel to the euro. Thus, a competition concept is set up between two currencies.

Violating on one hand, the EU-Contract (Art. 128 AEUV) and contradicting on the other, objectives of the European Community, solution discussion concepts

---

[9] See for this solution idea i.e. Meyer, D.: EURO-Krise. Austritt als Lösung, Berlin 2012, esp. pp. 26 - 33

[10] See i.e. Meyer, D.: EURO-Krise …, pp. 45 - 79

[11] See i.e. Meyer, D.: EURO-Krise …, pp. 33 - 43

[12] For calculation of the cost of exit of the euro system see Meyer, D.: EURO-Krise …, pp. 102 - 106

[13] See for discussion of the problematics of dual currencies i.e. Willms, M.: Zahlungsbilanz, Wechselkurs und Währungssysteme, in: Vahlens Kompendium der Wirtschaftstheorie und Wirtschaftspolitik, Vol. 1, 2nd ed., München 1984, pp. 215 – 253, here pp. 251 f.

have not been occurring as yet – this is incomprehensible. Agreements of all individual member states to do necessary changes in the contract is hardly to be expected.

Additionally, there is no direct effect to be expected on stability, neutrality, and counterfeit protection of the euro. It can more likely be assumed that according to the Gresham´s Law, more stable currencies could be pushed from the market from deteriorated (less stable) currencies.[14] Advantages of approval of parallel currencies would be avoided exits of member states from the euro system.

4. Dual Currency Union

Since exits of individual member states from the euro system have been associated with differently structured impacts to be estimated at different levels, common exits of larger groups of member states have been discussed. Specified groups should also have mutual currencies. This particular idea leads to dual divisions of the euro system – to dual currency unions. A north- and a south system has been under discussion. Consequently, there would be a north- and a south-euro.[15]

This dual division is a result of a geographic fact that northern states of the euro system would demonstrate a stronger stability in monetary- and currency policies than southern ones do.

This particular procedure could be compared with dividing soccer fields (compare fig. 14). Dividing the fields has been performed because in upper soccer field parts better teams have been playing. The lower part has been intended for the poorer teams. The specified division clarifies dividing the euro system in a north- and a south-euro.

Even a soccer-layman would immediately realize that dividing would not enable the "soccer game" of former times. Only one half of players would be available, new goals would be required, new field lines would be needed, an additional referee would be needed, etc. The "former" soccer game – as it has just been explained – would have been leading to the point of absurdity. Best solution would be: intensifying training of badly playing footballers and maintaining "former" soccer game rules.

---

[14] See to Gresham´s Law i.e. Fetter, F.W.: Gresham´s Law and the Chilean Peso, in: The Journal of Political Economy, Vol. 41 (1933), pp. 821 – 827; Bernholz, P.: Currency Competition. Inflation, Gresham´s Law and Exchange Rate, in: Zeitschrift für die gesamte Staatswissenschaft, Vol. 145 (1989), pp. 465 – 488; Selgin, G.: Salvaging Gresham´s Law: The Good, the Bad, and the Illegal, in: Journal of Money, Credit and Banking, Vol. 28 (1996), pp. 637 - 649

[15] See to this idea i.e. Henkel, H.O.: Rettet unser Geld, 3nd ed., München 2010. For critics see Eichengreen, B.: The Breakup of the Euro Area, http://eml.berkeley.edu/ called upon 12.16. 2014

Transferring this division proposal to the euro would mean that on one side, European Union objectives would not be fulfilled - that integration processes would be influenced and new institutions would have to be created. However, the most important argument against this particular solution is, that this specified division would clarify inabilities, solving true causes of the euro-crisis. The solution does not contribute directly to stability, neutrality, or counterfeit protection of the euro. The division of the currency can only be awarded indirect effects of stability.

Fig. 14: Comparison of the division of the euro with the analog division of a football field

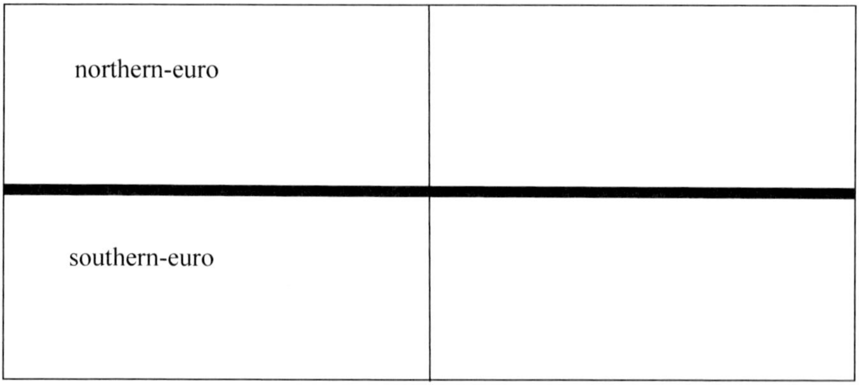

Source: own presentation

5. Euroization

"Euroization" is understood to be term for monetary- and currency policy proceedings of countries giving up their own national currencies and introducing – instead - the foreign currency "euro", as the legal tender.[16] Individual countries do not only give up their own national currencies, but also their independent monetary- and currency policies. Specified countries are neither members of euro states, nor in the European System of Central Banks, and nor represented in the European Central Bank. Euroization causes countries making themselves dependent from monetary- and currency policy situations of the Euro-States without being able to exert influence on monetary- and currency policies of these particular states. Otherwise, specified countries must not fulfill determined conditions of stability- and growth pacts respectively, the Six-Pack. Additionally, specified countries cannot be "punished" with sanctions in case of violations of Euro-State conditions.

---

[16] See i.e. Luchtmeier, H.: Dollarisierung und Euroisierung, Berlin 2005, esp. pp. 82 ff.

Monetary- and currency agreements with individual euro-states respectively European Union, must be preconditions for euroization. Such agreements with the European Union have been concluded – for example – by the Vatican State, Monaco, and San Marino.[17]

Otherwise, the European Union respectively Euro-States do not have any obligations supporting states with economic policy crisis having carried out euroization. For that particular reason, euroization has been seen as a possibility to avoid negative impacts on the euro security in introducing the euro in crisis-endangered states.

6. European Fiscal Union or Political Union

Foundation concepts of a European Fiscal Union have been discussed in this association.[18] Solving financial- and national debt issues in narrow collaboration frameworks member states of the European Union in a fiscal union has been achieved. The fiscal union requires the introduction of dues (taxes, fees, and contributions) on the EU-level. National states would have to transfer certain high volume taxes to the EU. Thus, national states would lose sovereignty. A centralizing effect would become apparent. Solving financial- and national debt issues could be dealt with, centrally. Introducing euro bonds could be seen in the introduction of the fiscal union to distribute solution measures on all member states.[19]

The idea of the political union being extended to a federal state is taking a step further.[20] Finally, there is hope to decrease differences among member states of the European Union responsible for financial- and national debt issues. Harmonization and integration have already been early-known prerequisites of functionalities of mutual/internal markets. The generous production factor transfer of (manpower, capital) can only be distortion-free (without any distortions), if all states concerned have the same conditions. This necessity has already been known at the time of the founding of the European Economic Community. A transitional period of 12 years was determined in the article of agreement for

---

[17] See Lamine, B.: Monetary and exchange-rate agreements between the European Community and Third Countries, European Commission Directorate-General for Economic and Financial Affairs, Economic Papers, N^0 255, Brussels 2006, pp. 33 – 35 (http://europa.eu.int/comm/economy-finance, called upon 07.09.2015)

[18] See i.e. Keuschnigg, C./Weyerstrass, K.: Sollte die EU eine Fiskalunion werden? In: Meyer, D. (Ed.): Die Zukunft der Währungsunion …, pp. 187 - 212

[19] See Keuschnigg, C./Weyerstrass, K.: Sollte die EU eine Fiskalunion werden? In: Meyer, D. (Ed.): Die Zukunft der Währungsunion …, p. 194

[20] The formation of a political union could possibly exceed the limits of European integration. See i.e. Franzius, C./Mayer, F.C./Neyer, J. (Ed.): Grenzen der europäischen Integration, Baden-Baden 2014; Scharf, F.: Die Finanzkrise als Krise der ökonomischen und rechtlichen Überintegration, in: Franzius, C./Mayer, F.C./Neyer, J. (Ed.): Grenzen der europäischen Integration, Baden-Baden 2014, pp. 51 - 60

harmonization at that particular time. Transitional period ended in the year 1969. However, a partial harmonization has only been reached. Instead of pushing harmonization, the Community/Union has been extended. That did not lead to any more harmonization. Above all, mutual market functionality – harmonizing market participant taxation is missing.

Some authors try to justify political unions as prerequisites for functional currency unions. Willgerodt[21] has examined historical, legal, and economic arguments for this particular thesis.

Fiscal- and/or political unions can only solve financial- and national debt issues by full harmonization as prerequisites for creating macro-economic equilibria in all member states. This statement is obvious for economic associations without applying great understandings. This specific issue is also accessible for everybody in the sport sector. Every European championship requires compliance with rules for all athletes of all nations. Every individual special regulation respectively deviation leads to unfair sport events.[22]

7. Conclusion

A closing evaluation of alternative proposals for solving euro-crisis could be based by dividing solution approaches into two groups. One of the groups consists of approaches deviating from actual objectives of the European Monetary Union and of a mutual currency – the euro. Approach of a northern- and a southern-euro is a component of this group. A mutual currency is necessary to create an integrated community in Europe with the objectives for peace and wealth. The second group of approaches does not neglect this particular objective. The European Stability Mechanism (ESM) is a component to this particular group. However, fulfillment of these approaches for creating functional mutual markets and mutual currencies are not necessarily being striven for.

Economic structures in all member states of the integration community must be totally harmonized to create peace and welfare in Europe. This is the condition for the freedom of movement of production factors in the community. Additionally, all economic units, all partial markets, and mutual total market quantity- and value related equilibria. The rule is – no crisis in the state of equilibria. Should additionally the proposed liberalization be accomplished, then there is no limit for an integration of member states. Furthermore, the euro is a secure currency on markets with quantity- and value related equilibria. Stability of the euro is at its highest at the quantity- and value related equilibrium. However, neutrality and counterfeit protection of the euro are not necessarily given at the equilibrium stages.

---

[21] See Willgerodt, H.: Politische Union als Voraussetzung einer Währungsunion? In: Neuere Entwicklungen in der Geldtheorie und Geldpolitik, ed. by Bofinger, P./Ketterer, K.-H., Tübingen 1996, pp. 137 – 163, esp. pp. 149 - 159

[22] See the football tail in Witte, H.: Die nachhaltige Marktwirtschaft, pp. 100 - 103

Part 6: Is there a Monetary System for a better Theoretical Basis than the Combination of Keynes Monetary Theory and Monetarism Available?

Currently practiced concepts to control national economies are comprised of – as it has just been presented above – two components: (1) money quantity- and (2) interest control. Quantity theory respectively monetarism, and the described theory by Keynes must be analyzed to test issues, whether there is a better theoretical basis of monetary policies for controlling national economies to be applied to. Should these particular weak points be demonstrated in theory, then these weak points must be improved by taking new approaches.

1. Interest Control Weaknesses

Interest control weaknesses have been demonstrated by monetarists. Interest controls effect economic processes with great time lags. Whenever the economy is at another developing phase stage (economic phase) interest changes can become effective. As a consequence, interest controls do not affect - as it would be desired – against development trends (anti-cyclical) but support undesired developments (pro-cyclical). Thus, controlling the national economy is unsuccessful.

2. Money Amount Control Weaknesses

First, weak points of money amount control should be identified to examine whether money amount controls are better on the theoretical basis than on monetarism; and then corrective measures should be developed. The three following weak points are in monetarism limiting effectiveness of a control of national economies by money quantities:

(a) Basic equation to money amount controls worked with velocity of money.

(b) Equation secures an equilibrium of money- and economic processes side of a national economy.

(c) Approach of money according to explanations of Friedman/Schwartz

(see above) only central bank money and cash are neutral.

To obliterate weak points – point (a) – it would be better to work with turnover rates, than with velocities of money. One step into the right direction is to operate with cash coefficients. However, this particular step is just to be valued as a weak successful approach because the cash coefficient (cc) is to be defined, as one divided by the velocity of money (V) (cc = 1/V).

A macro-economic equilibrium has to be created to obliterate weak point (b). Therefore partial markets of total markets – goods- and also labor markets have to be brought to an equilibrium. The basic equation has to be adjusted accordingly. Finally, to obliterate weak point (c) neutrality prerequisites of all partial money quantity components must be complied with. Total money amounts must be neutral.

The aggregates of the money amount M are presented in the following:[1]

M_1 =	cash (without cash balances of Banks) + sight deposits (daily maturing capital contributions) domestic non-Banks at credit institutions
M_2 =	M_1 + term deposits up to 2 years inland non-Banks at the credit institutions + deposits with an agreed upon notice period of up to 3 months
M_3 =	M_1, M_2 + repo transactions + shares in money business market fund shares as well as bonds up to 2 years

To obliterate the three weak points of money, a new equilibrium solution has to be developed.

3. Effects of Cash-Management Theory on Money Amount Control

Cash management theory has had quite a considerable influence on money amount controls because the basic equation - the Fisher Equation of Exchange and thus, also the later versions - have to be interpreted differently. Cash management theory operates with the cash coefficient better than with the velocity of money. Thus the Fisher Equation of Exchange adjusts itself to the following form:

(1) Money amount times one divided by the cash coefficient is equal to the barter volume.

Cash coefficient is the reciprocal value of velocity of money.

Formally this applies to:

(2) Velocity of money is equal to one divided by cash coefficient

For the newer version of the Fisher Exchange Equation with national income, gross domestic product (gross domestic income) respectively gross national product the following equations are obtained:

(3) Money amount times one divided by cash coefficient is equal to real national income times price level

(4) Money amount times one divided by cash coefficient is equal to gross national product (gross national income) times price level

(5) Money amount times one divided by cash coefficient is equal to gross domestic product times price level

[1] See Tab. 1 and Europäische Zentralbank: Monatsbericht Februar 1999, Frankfurt am Main 1999, p. 29

Cash management theories offer on one hand, other economic dimensions for determining money supplies than original quantity theory formulations. On the other hand, cash management theories activate above described deficiencies, this means the Fisher Equation of Exchange and following newer versions are not at all equations - considering measure units. Cash coefficients are - just as price levels – economic dimensions without measurement units; both sides of equations generate the same measurement units. However, cash coefficient definitions in equation (2) are not concluded. In this equation, measurement units are still the same because of cash coefficients - "unfortunately" - dependent on the velocity of money. Thus initial equations remain, despite logical approaches for improvements, continuously - inequalities.

4. Mistakes made by Money Amount Policy Introduction

Mistakes have been made by money amount control introductions: (1) A theoretically improved control of the economy with a higher stability – in other words, less inflation – has been introduced – however, without observing a long time planning period states and private social systems with high inflation rates. Consequently, these systems have faced difficulties. (2) Citizens – especially employers and managers – have not been "converted" to a stability policy. They have continued demanding annually increasing prices and high growth rates for companies as well as national economies. This type of behavior contradicts the stability policy.

Since theoretic guidelines have not necessarily been congruent, there have also been mistakes in handling money amount controls. This should be demonstrated in the following chapter based on the quantity theory and of theories set up by Keynes. Since criticisms should have been constructive basis for both opposing theories, approaches to formulate new approaches to control money supplies respectively national economies.

5. Money Amount Control According to Quantity Theory and Monetarism

Proposed controls of national economies by the quantity theory are based on the Fisher Exchange Equation. This particular equation creates an equilibrium between money- and goods-/real economical side of a national economy. This equation is perceived as an identity, since money- and goods-/real economical side of national economies have to be always equal (compare fig. 15).

Fig. 15: Equilibrium/Identity of money- and goods-/real economic sectors of a national economy

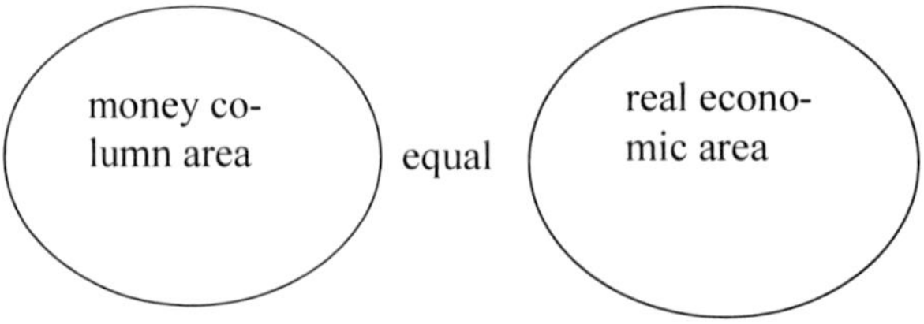

Source: own presentation

The Fisher Equation of Exchange states in its original version:[2]

(1) Money amount times velocity of money is equal to exchange volumes times price levels

Velocity of money is perceived as a shortly timed constant; equation can be simplified:

(2) Money amount is equal to exchange volume times price level

Both equations can be applied to national economy controls over money supplies. Control mechanisms generate from facts; money supplies can be smaller in a national economy than factors, resulting in multiplying exchange volumes and price levels, experiencing deflation. There is not enough money available to handle desired exchange-activities. Consequently, prices (the price levels) must be lowered to the point at which the available money supplies are sufficient, accomplishing desired exchange actions. This is the case when factors from exchange volumes and price levels are equal to money supplies. Deflation respectively price decreases avoid. However, market functionalities can also be solved by increasing money supplies, achieved by central banks. Thus, it demonstrates control mechanisms preventing market functionalities; deflation, and decreasing prices.

However, it is also possible to have greater money supplies than factors resulting in multiplying exchange volumes and price levels. There is more money in national economies than necessary for desired exchange actions. Market functionalities have not been influenced with this particular principle. All desired exchange actions can be performed.

Discussed is an inflation occurring at this situation. Prices (the price level) are increasing. Prices can be increased up to the point where money supplies correspond to factors of exchange volumes and price levels. According to above identified control mechanisms, central banks have now to decrease money supplies up to the point in which factors from money supplies are equal to factors com-

[2] See Fisher, I.: The Purchasing Power of Money, New York 1911, pp. 24 – 28, 47 – 49, 53 – 54, 149 - 183

posed of exchange volumes and price levels to prevent inflation respectively increasing prices. This particular mechanism has also been used, according to the quantity theory.

However, inflation cannot explain proposed control mechanisms respectively additional money amount increases. It is different in the case of deflation. To maintain market functionalities; deflation must occur. It can be prevented by increasing money supplies provided by central banks. Principally, inflation must not occur with huge money supplies, because money supplies do not influence market functionalities. Consequently, increased money supplies cannot be the cause for inflation observed in practice. There must be other, or differentiated causes.[3] However, excessive money supplies allow price increases because desired exchange actions have made them possible. Thus, control mechanisms can be applied to money amount decreases to prevent inflation. Money supplies must be decreased up to the factor in which exchange volumes and price levels correspond to each other.

Success of money amount controls are greater at the deflation side than at the inflation side – as perceived by an attentive observer. Since deflation has been caused by too low money supplies available, considering the performance, cause for inflation – but small money supplies. Partial success of money amount control has led to appropriate criticism. Keynes has been considered as one of the most vehement critic of the quantity theory and of the included money amount control theory represented. However, criticism on money amount controls has not led to the Keynesian theory but also to adjustments of the Fisher Exchange Equation. Different modern versions have been developed.

Adjustments of the Fisher Equation of Exchange for the improvement of money amount controls have taken place above all by the substantiation of exchange- respectively trade volumes. The real national income can be set up in the equation instead of the exchange volume. The national income is equal to the net national product to the factor costs. It is calculated in subtracting the amortizations from the gross national product to the market prices (net national product to market prices). Then, in subtracting the indirect taxes and adding the subsidies the net national product to factor costs or rather the national income is the result. Furthermore, the cash management coefficient, the reciprocal value calculated applied in the calculation – instead of with the velocity of the money, the result is an equation (3) – known as the Cambridge Equation:

(3) Money amount is equal to cash coefficient times price level times real national income

[3] The different reasons for inflation are not mentioned here. See i.e. Riese, H.: Theorie der Inflation, Tübingen 1986, pp. 80 – 172; Ströbele, W.: Inflation, 4th ed., München, Wien 1995, pp. 42 - 90

Using gross national products is a further possibility to adjust the Fisher Exchange Equation. Then it generates the Equation (4) presented version of the Fisher Exchange Equation:[4]

(4) Money amount times velocity of money is equal to gross national product

Gross national product includes all active sales in a national economy. Sales are estimated at market prices. One may also refer to gross national products of market prices. In calculating gross national products, preliminary work, that is – subtraction of purchases achieved at other companies – avoiding double counting. Gross national products have to be equalized with the performance of only the domestic people (domestic product).

However, this equation does not convince critics because money supplies refer to official currencies of states, valid for sovereign territories. However, gross national products are not referred to individual areas – respectively individual regions but to individual persons (the domestic individuals). However, there is no homonymy possible.

Calculation has to be performed with gross domestic products referred to gross domestic products of sovereign territories to create homonymy. Gross domestic products are obtained by adding the income of gross national products of individual foreigners and the income from domestic individuals living in foreign countries and subtracting them from gross national products. Individual domestic persons living in foreign countries and foreign individuals living in this country are thereby considered. Inserting– instead of the exchange-/trade volume respectively gross national product the gross domestic product into the original version of the Fisher Exchange Equation, the following equation (5) is obtained:

(5) Money times velocity of money is equal to gross domestic product times price level

Equation (4) and (5) can also function – instead of applying velocity of money with reciprocal value - the cash management coefficient.

It does not depend - to what extent - the logic of the connection between the two sides of the values of these particular dimensions of the alternative dimensions for the exchange volume and velocity of money. Differences between appropriate values according to official statistics are clear.[5] Thus the following argumentation seems to be important.

Interpretation of the Fisher Equation of Exchange and its newer versions demonstrate, that the left side of the equation constantly achieves the money amount of the equation and then the money demand on the right side of the equation, consisting of the exchange-, trade volume, gross national product

---

[4] See Woll, A.: Quantitätstheorie, in: Handwörterbuch der Wirtschaftswissenschaft (HdWW), 6. Vol., Stuttgart, New York a.o. 1981, pp. 392 – 399, esp. pp. 394 f.

[5] See Tab. 8

(gross national income) respectively gross domestic product or national income. Therefore, monetary markets are partly presented on each individual side of the equation, whereas goods-, employment-, and information markets are summarized and designated at the right side of the equation, in which money demands have been identified. Consequently, different versions of the Fisher Equation of Exchange do not secure equilibria on goods-, employment-, information-, and monetary markets. When there is neither deflation nor inflation present, then it is only the equilibrium (or rather an identity) of money- and real economic side respectively money supplies and money demands, identified in a national economy guaranteeing equilibria on markets. The equation must be formulated in more detail, securing equilibria for all partial markets. This shall be further discussed in paragraph 7 of Part 6 (see below).

To evaluate money amount performances controls, according to concepts of the quantity theory, is to discuss individual dimensions in basic equations – the Fisher Exchange Equation.

Money amount M_3 has been prevailing as a control parameter. Considering components of the money amount M_3 (compare Tab. 1), it can be seen that the majority part of this particular money amount is not neutral in the light of the foregoing of Newlyn and Friedman (compare paragraph 2 of Part 3). It is only component cash, ranked as neutral by mentioned authors. It must be concluded, that one important prerequisite for currency euro security has not been met yet.

Since velocity of money as well as price level can be equal to one – it should be examined whether money amount M_3 definitions, gross domestic product definitions, respectively gross national income definitions (a new term for gross national product) and of the national income are appropriate.

Limitations of the four terms are presented in tab. 6. Values from official statistics for the year 2013 demonstrate that the four terms have not yet been identified with the same values. Gross national products have the highest values. Gross domestic products, the money amount M_3, and the national income follow.

Calculation of velocity of money (respectively turnover of money) would lead the identified value for the money amount M_3 to different values.

Calculation of velocity of money supported by gross national income results in a value of rounded up by two digits to 1.21. However, corresponding values for gross domestic products and the national income are 1.18 as well as 0.97.[6]

Should identified values for the gross national income in tab. 6, gross national income, gross domestic product, and national income be considered in calculating the money amount M_3, regarding a short termed constant velocity of money (i.e. of one), one would obtain different values for the money amount M_3. Then the money amount M_3 is at first 2,813.8 Bill. Euro and then finally 2,127.9 Bill.

---

[6] Own calculations based on values from Tab. 8.

euro.; then 2,737.6 Bill. euro. The result is not the specified one, identified in municipal statistics of a value of 2,319.4 Bill. euro.

The identified values in table 6 of presented calculation examples, clarify the difficulty performing exact money amount controls and demonstrate the importance of optimum reference parameters for the Fisher Equation of Exchange respectively a variant of this particular equation.

Tab. 8: Comparison of limitations of money amount M_3, gross domestic product, gross national income, and national income

components of the money amount M_3	components of the gross domestic product	components of the gross national income	components of the national income
cash (without the cash assets of the banks)			
demand deposits (daily deposits due) domestic non-banks at credit institutions	production value of all products minus preliminary work produced in one economic period in the inland	gross domestic product plus the accounting balance of the primary income with the rest of the world	gross national income minus write offs minus production- and import
term deposits below 4 years of domestic non-banks at the credit institutions	plus product taxes minus goods subsidies n (= value of all domestically produced end products)		taxes to the state plus governmental subsides
2,319.4 Bill. euro	2,737.6 Bill. euro	2,813.8 Bill. Euro	2,127.9 Bill. Euro
Values 2013 to the individual prices for the Federal Republic of Germany			

Source: own presentation according to Brümmerhoff, D./Grömling, M.: Volkswirtschaftliche Gesamtrechnungen, 9th ed., München 2011, pp. 1, 55; Statistisches Bundesamt (Ed.): Statistisches Jahrbuch. Deutschland und Internationales, Wiesbaden 2014, p. 321; Deutsche Bundesbank: Monatsbericht Februar 2015, 67. Jg., No. 2, Frankfurt am Main 2015, p. 13*

The second component of the Fisher Equation of Exchange respectively its different versions is velocity of money. Velocity of money assures that the Fisher Equation of Exchange and its newer versions consider measurement units of individual parameters without equations but inequalities. Velocity is always measured as a traveled distance per time unit. On one side, it does not make any sense to multiply the measured money amount with the distance per time. The resulting measurement unit is still unknown - it is also nonsense. Secondly, measured gross national products (gross national income) or gross domestic products on the right side are multiplied with the index without the measurement unit price level. Thus, on the left equation side, a contrasting measurement unit is obtained compared with the right side.

Rectifying this contradiction and adjusting the Fisher Equation of Exchange actually to an equation, velocity of money must be processed – instead - with the turnover rate of money. The turnover rate of money is also measured as the index – without a measurement unit. Thus, equality of measurement units is given on both of sides after multiplying referred parameters. Thus, an equation is achieved.

The idea working with the turnover rate of money is supported by the example of needed amount of money, purchasing a pizza, in the textbook by Mankiv/Taylor.[7] But also older texts by Cassels[8] have supported the idea.

Cash management coefficients have to be identified as turnover resistances.

Forecast of controls of money supplies respectively national economy is independent from criticisms of measurement units. Money supplies must be provided on monetary markets on time if any exchange activities should be taking place. First, however, exchange volumes (real national income, gross national product, gross domestic product) and price levels must be predicted.

Actually many methods have been provided in literature for forecasts for differently designed time series (among others for regular and irregular processes of time series). It will always remain a problem performing forecast errors. An underestimation leads to provisions of understated money supplies and consequently, it will be impossible to perform certain exchange activities. A deflation tendency could occur. However, deflation is undesired. Consequently, a security factor has to be installed so that money supplies are always excessive to process all exchange activities.

Minimizing forecast errors, by testing the less known forecast methods developed by Holt[9], whether different fluctuation forms and different fluctuation type combinations would lead to improved forecast results and therefore enable a more accurate control of money amount.

Concluding, advantages of money amount controls have greater and quicker influences on the economy than interest rate controls. However, a few disadvantages are opposing: (1) Only a partial component with non-interest and therefore it is neutral, (2) no consideration of partial markets of total markets, and (3) there are definition issues to formulate control equations as well as forecast issues in determining values for parameters contained in equations.

---

[7] See Mankiv, N.G./Taylor, M.P.: Grundzüge der Volkswirtschaftslehre, p. 742

[8] See Cassel, G.: Theoretische Sozialökonomie, p. 401

[9] See Holt, C.C.: Forecasting seasonals and trends by exponentially weighted moving averages, in: International Journal of Forecasting, Vol. 20 (2004), pp. 5 - 10

6. Interest Control According to Model set up by Keynes

Developed theories by Keynes have led – well-known – equilibria at situations of underemployment. Interest control results from the formula for equilibria on goods markets. Planned savings are - according – to this equation (equation 6) equal to investments. Savings dependent on national incomes. Investments dependent on interest rates. Interest rate changes influence investments. They again have influences on economic affairs processes.

The theory set up by Keynes is graphically demonstrated in fig. 16. Fig.16 clearly shows money- and goods market equilibria – while disequilibria (unemployment) are existing on labor markets.

Fig. 16: Equilibria of money- and goods markets at disequilibria on labor markets

Source: own presentation

Basic equations for formulating equilibria on goods-, money-, and labor markets are presented in the equations (6) to (9).[10]

(6) planned savings equal to planned investments

When savings are equal to investments – equilibria on goods markets are given. Money market equilibria are formulated in equation (7):

(7) money amount is equal to money demand

When money amount is equal to money demand then there is an equilibrium on the money market.

Money demand is price level times demand, according to real balances – depending on national income and interest rate.

Labor market equilibrium is given in the following equation (8):

(8) labor demand equal to labor offer

When equal labor offers are equal to labor demands, then there is an equilibrium on the labor market. Labor offers depend on real-wages obtained by dividing

[10] See Keynes, J.M.: Allgemeine Theorie ..., pp. 20 – 29, 33 – 40, 46 – 57, 77 – 91, 140 – 147, 168 – 172, 237 – 244, 257 – 259; see also the transparent and short presentation by Siebert, H.: Einführung in die Volkswirtschaftslehre, 9th ed., Stuttgart a.o. 1989, p. 254

nominal wages by price levels. Labor offers can be seen short termed respectively simplified constants. Labor demands depend on demands on goods markets – respectively from real wages and national income. Unemployment is achieved by the difference of labor offers and labor demands. Thus Keynes has arrived at a further equation (9) for equilibria on labor markets, including unemployment (underemployment):

(9) labor demand plus unemployment is equal to labor offer

Demand for labors has been achieved by macro-economic production functions. Macro-economic production functions determine national income. National income is determined by production functions. National income is a function of labor demands. An equilibrium is given when both parameters are equal:

(10) National income is equal to a function of labor demand

Equations (6 - 10) set up by Keynes are principally simple and comprehensible. Interesting would be, evaluating this particular equation, whether it could convince to be a basis for controlling the national economy.

Striking is the definition of goods market equilibria – as planned - savings equalizing planned investments. This particular definition deviates from definitions of equilibria for money- and labor markets. Keynes has directly based money- as well as labor markets on equilibrium offers and demands. Planned savings and planned investments do not directly represent goods offers - neither goods on demand. Furthermore, these savings must rather be allocated to the money- than to the goods markets.

Keynes has adopted unemployment directly into the definition equation. Thus, formulating macro-economic equilibria at the stage of underemployment is definition-adopted and not a conclusion. However, the viewpoint to macro-economic equilibria in which important partial markets are present at disequilibria must be discussed. It should be pointed out, that there are no macro-economic equilibria in the sense of Walras[11] available.

Furthermore, should be noted - as it has been mentioned above - all parameter forecast issues are present. Regarding this, approaches of Keynes have not offered any improvements. Improvements have affected the quantity theory confronting Keynes, in considering three important partial markets of total markets. Keynes has set up equilibrium conditions for all three partial markets. The quantity theory does not do this - assumed is an equilibrium of a money- and goods economy side of a national economy. This specified relationship has been known as an identity.

Formulated equations by Keynes for equilibria on goods- and labor markets do not convince at all. Thus Keynes has not actually issued an improvement regard-

[11] See Walras, L.: Elements d´économie politique pure ou théorie de la richesse sociale, Lausanne, Paris, Bale (Basel) 1874, pp. 112 – 118, 126 - 131

ing control of a national economy. Since Keynes's developed concept controlling the national economy, it has nevertheless had a long-termed dominant influence on the economic theory and – policy. Approaches to the quantity theory have become - intermediate at least - for practical economy policies less significant. Application of both approaches on practical economy policies have just been changed again by a new formulation of the quantity theory – monetarism. The new quantity theory has prevailed, without referring to improvements by Keynes. Monetarism has not considered partial markets either. Only basic equations by substituting parameters for parameters have led to determining volumes of exchange activities. The new basic equation only continues to take account in individual equilibria of money- and goods economic sides of a national economy. It still relies on an individual identity. Principally, the above stated criticism on the quantity theory has still maintained. Corrections to control the national economy are insufficient to carry out successful controls. Actually, money is currently dominating practical economic policies respectively monetary- and currency policies. However, economic crisis cannot be prevented. They have been occurring at shorter intervals. Thus, further improvements for control mechanisms are urgently needed.

Corrections could be attempted by approaching the quantity theory respectively money as well as to the approach of Keynes. Basics improved approaches to control a national economy are discussed in the two following paragraphs. The importance of a new equation to control a national economy tied up in the Szczecin Equation[12] is to be demonstrated. Additionally, a macro-economic equilibrium will be discussed – considering all partial markets of a total market. Assumed are equilibria for all partial markets. The forecast issue will be discussed in the following paragraphs.

In conclusion, advantages and disadvantages from approaches developed by Keynes are to be summarized, one more time. Approach advantages are considering partial markets of total markets. Additionally, determining the national income and thus, demand for labor for macro-economic production functions are convincing.

Disadvantage is that equations for goods markets - and for labor market equilibria are not really convincing. Additionally, interest controls are not as effective as controls for money supplies because of existing time lags. With the approach developed by Keynes, it is only the interest dependent component of money amount to be controlled. This greater part of money supplies is, according to monetarists not neutral and does not guarantee stability (see above). The dependent part from income of money amount has not been discussed by Keynes.

---

[12] See Witte, H.: Die Szczecin-Gleichung, in: Witte, H.: The Szczecin School of „simple“ Economics, Szczecin 2010, pp. 35 - 44

7. Own Approach to Money Control Based on Value Related Production Function

Developing a new approach to control the national economy through money supplies is to connect advantages of the quantity theory to obtain an improvement of current control mechanisms.

Advantages of the quantity theory respectively money are in control of the national economy through money supplies instead of interest rates. Changes of money amount effects are clearly faster achieved and are anti-cyclic whereas the variation of interest rates are obtained later and are pro-cyclical.

Advantages of Keynes's approach are - in considering the three important partial markets of the total markets - money-, goods-, and labor markets. Furthermore, deviating formal relationships from macro-economic production functions have been convincing.

Approaches to be developed are consequently based on setting up equilibria relationships for money-, goods-, and labor markets deviated from macro-economic production functions. An equilibrium of all three partial markets is to be formulated (compare fig. 17).

By an existing equilibrium in quantity- as well as value-based situation a "real" equilibrium must be considered on markets for deviating equilibrium relationships. Only a quantity- or - only a value-based equilibrium cannot simultaneously be transferred into an equilibrium situation. Consequently, a value-based and not a quantity-based macro-economic production function must be applied for deviating equilibrium relationships.

At first sight deviating equilibrium relationships of the Cobb-Douglas-Production-Function offers itself. It is probably the best known and most often used function of many known macro-economic production functions. The Cobb-Douglas-Production-Function is to be ranked as a mixed production function. Labor is achieved quantity-based in this function and capital is value-based. Since different measurement units cannot be calculated together, conversion of index values must be obtained - according to Cobb and Douglas – without a measurement unit ("..., it is of course necessary to construct indexes of the relative amounts of labor and capital ..."[13]). Since index values do not allow a determination of value-based equilibria, a macro-economic production function must be applied.

A value-based production function leading to the same result after converting a value- into a quantity-based result has been achieved - it is the following simple value-based production. This production function is at first formulated for a

[13] Cobb, C.W./Douglas, P.H.: A Theory of Production, in: American Economic Review, Vol. XVIII (1928), Supplement, pp. 139 – 165, here p. 140

company and can then later on be aggregated onto all companies of a macro-economic production functions of the same type.[14] This particular production function is:

(11) revenue is equal to costs

Insertion of this simple value-based production function, in accordance with the parameters of the Cobb-Douglas-Production Function to be considered - costs of labor (LC) and costs of capital (CAC), the following formulation is obtained:[15]

(12) revenue is equal to costs of work plus costs of capital

The following formulation results from the macro-economic production function:

(13) gross national product is equal to revenues from all transactions

respectively

(14) gross national product is equal to costs of labor plus costs of capitals of all transactions

At first, all companies and staff of companies must be in a quantity- and value-based equilibria if equilibria is to be created on goods markets on the basis of this particular production function. Companies are in quantity- and value-based equilibria when companies produce exactly the demanded quantities of goods (offers equalize demands, quantity-based equilibria) and revenues correspond exactly to costs for labor and costs for capital (value-based equilibria):

(15) amount equalizing demand quantity

and

(16) revenue equalizing costs of labor plus costs of capital

All staff of individual companies must be in equilibria situations - to guarantee this the equations (15) and (16) are to be applied. However, they must be reworded for the staff with convincing parameters. The first equation can be applied without rewording. Each individual staff member is at a quantity-based equilibrium if he is in the following relationship:

(17) quantity demand of each individual staff member equalizing per member (per individual) the offered quantity of goods

Wages of each individual staff member must equalize expenditures of individual to secure value-based equilibria for each staff member:

(18) wage for each individual staff member equalizing expenditures of each individual. A simple example is to demonstrate equilibrium conditions.

---

[14] See Witte, H.: The Monetary Production Function as a Basis of Sustainability, in: edited by Witte, H. a.o.: Sustainable Logistics, Bahia Blanca 2012, pp.13 – 23, esp. pp. 14, 17 - 22

[15] The production function is derived out of the equation for efficiency.

Assumed is a small national economy with just one company and two citizens. Both citizens work in this particular insular company. One of them plays the role as a worker and the other one is the capital owner. The company produces a vital necessity every staff member has to buy to survive. The equilibrium conditions for this case are demonstrated in the following table (compare table 9).

Recognized from tab. 9 is that the company has to produce two quantity units from essentially necessary goods and it can also sell them. Consequently, the company is in a quantity-based equilibrium situation. At first price of the good is to be determined to create a value-based equilibrium. Assumed are alternative prices 1, 2, 3, 4, and 5 euros. Achieved is - accordingly - a revenue (revenue equalizing the price times sold quantity) of 2, 4, 6, 8, and 10 euro. Revenues must be equal to costs to obtain value-based equilibria. Distributing these costs to the costs for labor (wages of worker) and costs for capital (salary of capital owner) so that each individual citizen/staff member can exactly buy life essential quantities of goods – one arrives at a wage of 1, 2, 3, 4, and 5 euros.

Tab 9: Equilibrium conditions for a small insular economy

number of citizens	quantity units of the good	price of good	revenue = price x quantity	costs	Σ wages	wage/employee
2	2	0	0	0	0	0
2	2	1	2	2	2	1
2	2	2	4	4	4	2
2	2	3	6	6	6	3
2	2	4	8	8	8	4
2	2	5	10	10	10	5

Source: own presentation

Thus, equilibrium conditions can be formulated in the following way:

(19) quantity units of goods equalize number of citizens (staff members)

(20) price per quantity equalizing wage per staff member

The condition in equation (19) secures a quantity-based equilibrium and the equation (20) secures a value-based equilibrium onto goods markets.

Additionally, equilibrium conditions for labor markets are results from tab. 7:

(21) number of labors equal to number of citizens

(22) wages per individual staff member equal to price per quantity units

Finally, equilibrium conditions for monetary markets can be derived from tab. 9:

(23) money amount equalizing price times quantity unit

or

(24) money amount equalizing revenue

respectively

(25) money amount equalizing wage sum

respectively

(26) money amount equal to the wage per staff member times number of staff members

Money amount corresponds to money quantity. Demand for money corresponds to revenue or rather wage sum. All necessary transactions can be carried out in this particular small national economy with a money amount of 2, 4, 6, 8, and 10 euro because a demand for money with 2, 4, 6, 8, and 10 euro is appropriate to the money amount. Demonstrated equilibrium conditions secure quantity- and value-based. Equilibria are appropriate to each other and secure macro-economic quantity- and value-based equilibria. Connection is demonstrated graphically in fig. 17.

Fig 17: Equilibrium of money-, goods-, and labor market

Source: own presentation

The model of the small insular national economy was needed to derive the equilibrium conditions for a national economy in a simple and comprehensible method. Issue now is to examine whether or not the found equilibrium conditions are also valid for a large national economy. This question is to be answered with "yes". Alternative prices have been applied in tab. 1 and equilibrium conditions have been demonstrated that equilibrium conditions are not only valid for one price. In accordance, number of the citizens, number of companies, and number of goods can be changed as desired. Should assumed framework conditions be still valid, the assumed relationship between parameters are considered to maintain constancy, then there will always be logical equilibrium solutions confirming achieved price regulations. The logic is so simple and obvious that it does not need any confirmation for a stimulation.

Found equilibrium conditions form improved basis for controlling national economies through money quantity controls.

The small national insular economy is surely not the case to be met often in practice. Recognized from tab. 1 equilibrium, conditions do not only lead to equilibria with alternative prices to equilibria. Regarding number of citizens' small national economy can extend numbers of companies and goods as desired. In maintaining found equilibrium conditions, equilibria can also be created in large national economies.[16]

7.1 Detailed Consideration of Goods Market

Goods markets are subdivided into markets for material goods, for services, for nominal goods, and for markets for information. An equilibrium on goods markets must secure that all of these partial markets of goods market must be in equilibria. Above presented equilibrium conditions secure quantity- and value-based equilibria on all partial markets of goods-, but also on money-, and on labor markets. This is achieved by deriving the below presented equilibrium conditions on the basis of equilibria of companies and staffs. Presented in fig. 18 are methods of quantity- and quality-based equilibria required on goods markets to secure goods market equilibria.

Fig. 18: Equilibrium of goods market

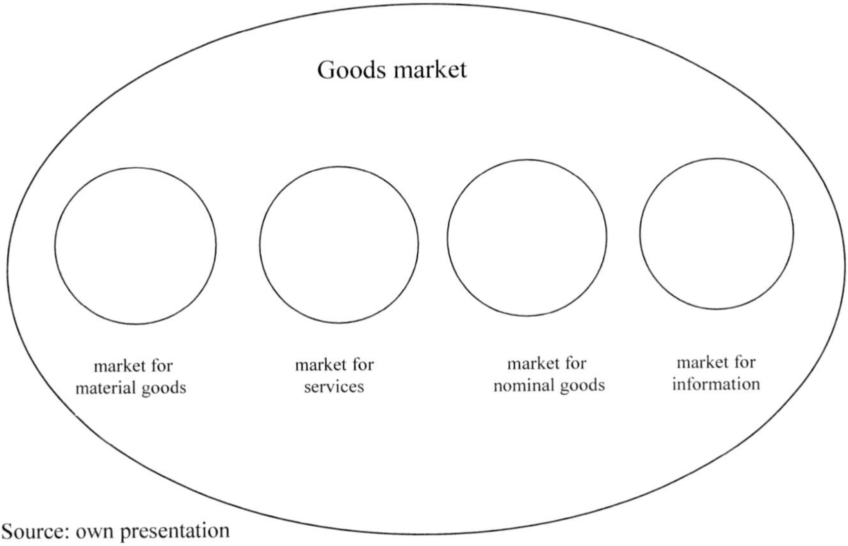

Source: own presentation

[16] For presentation of enlarged models see Witte, H.: Die nachhaltige Marktwirtschaft, pp. 127 - 143

7.2 Forecast of Money Amount

Money supplies for the money amount control provided by central banks on markets must be predicted before exchange activities can take place. Consequently first, exchange- respectively trade volume is to be predicted. Exchange volumes are currently determined according to new versions of the Fisher Equation of Exchange based on the gross domestic product or the national income. In other words, gross domestic products or national incomes must be predicted first. There are two methods for this forecast. First method is direct forecast of gross domestic products or national incomes. A second, somewhat more elaborate, is predicting both values over macro-economic production functions containing components influencing considerably both values.

Both methods are to be discussed. At first, general forecast issues are to be described.

7.2.1 General Forecast Issue

The general forecast issue includes estimating forecast values at the point of time – today – for the future, on a basis of values based on past values assisted by a forecast method (compare fig. 19). Since past values demonstrate a specific process, they represent a selectable forecast for taking into account past processes of values. According to multiple cases for the process of past values, a multitude of forecast methods has been formulated in literature.

Fig. 19: The forecast

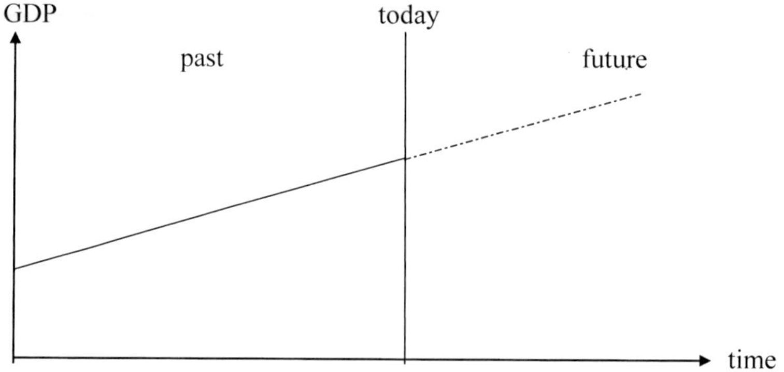

Source: own presentation

Generally, it has been differentiated between regular and irregular (sporadic) processes of past values. Regular processes have been described as individual values located at each point of time in the past. Should not every individual point of time be located at each individual past point, an irregular process is consequently to be discussed. Both general processes could be subdivided into subforms. At first there is a constant process. Whenever values are equal at every individual point of time, there is a constant process occurring. Minor deviations or rather fluctuations are to be considered because there are hardly any constant processes of values in practice. A second case is the process of past values with increasing trends. Also in this particular case there are minor deviations from trends – thus, fluctuations accepted - in other words - to be able to discuss a further linear increasing trend. The third subset of processes of past values are seasonal fluctuations. Values fluctuate on seasonal basis in both deviation directions. These three subsets of past process values have been generally distinguished for forecasts and appropriate methods have been offered taking into account initial past values for forecasts. However, cases of combined process values with trends and seasonal fluctuations have not been considered so often in literature up to now. Correspondingly rare have forecast methods been discussed satisfying these process forms. Combined forecast methods developed by Holt serve as an example.[17]

All forecast methods have parameters enabling adjustments to data situations. At first ex-post-forecasts with past values are accomplished, selecting and adjusting forecast parameters. "Ex-ante" forecasts and selected parameter values are set up, only when predicted values coincide with realized past values. Comparisons are impossible with actually realized values at forecast points of time. Comparisons of realized values can be achieved only when forecast horizons have been accomplished. However, at that particular point of time forecast value improvements are too late. Forecasts have either been described as being good or bad.

7.2.2 Forecast Issues of Money Amount

Three alternative methods to predict money supplies are available: (1) predicted future money supplies directly from past money supplies, (2) predicted are future money supplies indirectly attracted or (3) predicted are money supplies indirectly by predicting future gross domestic products with macro-economic production functions and both production factors - work and capital. In this case future gross domestic products are predicted from past parameter values - labor and capital.

Methods (1) and (2) correspond approximately to work input, whereas method (3) is clearly more complex because two parameters have to be estimated resulting in gross domestic products and thus resulting in necessary money supplies. Since assumed, more detailed context considerations have been achieved, this third method could possibly provide improved forecast values. Finally, qualities can only be estimated in completed empirical comparisons with these three presented methods – however, this was impossible in this particular framework.

[17] See Holt, C.C.: Forecasting seasonals and trends by exponentially weighted moving averages, pp. 5 - 10

7.3 Determining the Turnover Rate of Money

Exact determination of turnover rates of money is for calculating money supplies of a fundamental importance. Inactive determinations of turnover rates of money lead to miscalculations of money supplies and therefore to inaccurate money amount controls. Avoiding inflation or deflation is consequently suboptimal. Definition of turnover rate of money is one important prerequisite for accurate determinations of turnover rates of money. Having solved the definition issue suitable calculation methods have to be developed. At first, calculation methods should be discussed – regularly applied – determining turnover rates - respectively velocity of money.

Generally, the Fisher Equation of Exchange respectively a variant of this particular equation is discussed – it has already been presented as equation (5) above.

(5) Money amount times velocity of money is equal to gross domestic product times price level

Determining turnover of money respectively velocity of money, the equation according to this particular parameter is then dissolved (27):

(27) Velocity of money is equal to product from gross domestic product and price level divided by money amount

However, determining velocity- or rather turnover of money based on equation (27), results with a problem. Since generally, money supplies are determined with assumptions of short timed constant velocities respectively turnover rates determining velocities respectively turnover rates are self-dependent. Since solutions with two unknowns are unsolvable, results cannot be convincing. Consequentially, other methods have to be developed, determining velocities- respectively turnover rates of money. This particular method is to be found by the turnover rate of money.

Difficulty defining velocity of money has been described by – among other authors - Lutz.[18] He has contrasted opinions of two author groups. For one group there just has not been the issue of velocity of money because it does not have any influence on price levels. Consequently, each individual money circulation has a relationship to a goods circulation. Both changes compensate each other. The other author group sees turnover rate of money as well as money amount as equally effective, because increase of velocity of money has the same impact on price levels as increase of money supplies.[19]

---

[18] See Lutz, F.: Über die Umlaufgeschwindigkeit des Geldes, in: Jahrbücher für Nationalökonomie und Statistik, Vol. 144 (1936), pp. 385 – 409, here pp. 385 f.; see also Holtrop, M.W.: Die Umlaufgeschwindigkeit des Geldes, in: Hayek, F.A. (Ed.): Beiträge zur Geldtheorie, Wien 1933 (reprint Berlin a.o. 2007, pp. 115 – 209)

[19] See Lutz, F.: Über die Umlaufgeschwindigkeit des Geldes ..., p. 386

Presented are possible causal relationships between turnover rate of money (TR) and money supplies, gross domestic products as well as price levels in tab. 10. Twelve different cases of possible causal relationships are differentiated.

Tab. 10: Causal relationship between turnover rates of money and money supplies, gross domestic products as well as price levels

case 1	TR = 0	AM = 0	GDP = 0	P = 0
case 2	TR → ∞	AM → = 0	GDP = ?	P = ?
case 3	TR↑	AM↓	GDP = constant	P = constant
case 4	TR↑	AM↓	GDP↑	P↑
case 5	TR↑	AM↓	GDP↓	P↑
case 6	TR↑	AM↓	GDP↑	P↓
case . 7	TR↑	AM↓	GDP↓	P↓
case 8	TR↓	AM↑	GDP = constant	P = constant
case 9	**TR↓**	**AM↑**	**GDP↑**	**P↑**
case 10	TR↓	AM↑	GDP↓	P↑
case 11	TR↓	AM↑	GDP↑	P↓
case 12	TR↓	AM↑	GDP↓	P↓

Source: own presentation

Only possible causal relationships are presented in tab. 10. A statement about strength of individual effects and their compensations has not been made. Downward directed arrows imply a decrease of appropriate parameters whereas upward directed ones emphasize an increase. Case 9 is to be referred to explaining today's situation. Increase of money amount, gross domestic product, and price level are caused by a decrease in turnover rates of money.[20]

Having demonstrated possible causal relationships of turnover rates of money with money supplies, turnover rates of money (respectively velocities of money) have to be defined. Cassel[21] has emphasized the term (velocity of money) as a rule, has not been clearly presented in detail yet. Since the term has to be defined relating to one specified economic period - according to his point of view, not only money supplies but also reference to payments must be considered, as well as every coin used in specified economic periods. Assumed is that all coins have been considered used equally frequent in a specified economic period. Then the extent of ongoing payments is equal to available money supplies of possible payments in one specified economic period.

[20] Compare the falling velocity of money in the tables and figures in Annex 2.

[21] See Cassel, G.: Theoretische Sozialökonomie ..., p. 401

However, since the coins have not been spent equally frequent, payments of available money supplies are equal to payments of individual coins. Cassel[22] has determined the average turnover rate of money (velocity of money), assumed is that money supplies are constant in given specified economic periods. He has multiplied the nominal value of all coins with the number of all processed payments – these values have been summed up and divided by the new value (total value of the processed payments) by money supplies:

(28) average turnover rate is equal to sum of nominal value of all coins times number of achieved payments divided by money supplies

Another definition of velocity (respectively turnover rate) of money can be found by Lutz. Lutz defines velocity of money from the viewpoint of an individual-[23] and a macro-economic[24] view. Individual economic cash balances are equal to average cash balances in the national economy if money supplies are constant in the specified economic period. Determining velocity of money from the point of view of macro-economic comprehends velocity of money of the national economy. Lutz based his assumption on the exchange equation and determines average cash balances big enough to process all exchange activities at a specified price level. Average cash balances are equal to sums of added individual cash balances and equal to money supplies in the national economy.

Comparing different definitions of velocities of money with other written ones in literature thus far, it has been found that there have been various parameters playing a role for a specified definition. According to Cassel, this is the denomination of the coins in individual coins, bank notes as well as their turnover rates, frequencies of usage for payments in one specified economic period. According to Lutz, individual- and macro-economic cash balances respectively money supplies for the definition of velocity of money of importance. Since cash balances depend on income, individual- and macro-economic income play also a role.

It should be referred to the here found definition of turnover rate of money to different economic situations. It is a definition of turnover rate of money developing an equilibrium- and a disequilibrium situation.

[22] See Cassel, G.: Theoretische Sozialökonomie …, p. 401

[23] See. Lutz, F.: Über die Umlaufgeschwindigkeit des Geldes …, pp. 386 f.

[24] See Lutz, F.: Über die Umlaufgeschwindigkeit des Geldes …, p. 388

7.3.1 Determining the Turnover Rate of Money in Equilibrium

At first a definition for the turnover of money for equilibrium situations has been developed. All economic units spend their complete income in a specified economic period during the same specified economic period in equilibrium situations. There is neither saving nor are there any credits given in this situation.

The complete income can be seen as cash balance. Judging from the definition of turnover rate of money from the cash balance according to Lutz, turnover rate of money must be presented by 'one', since each individual economic unit can spend its income only once per specified economic period – and it is also performed in that particular way. Turnover rate of money is equal to one is just logical – according to Cassel's definition, assuming spending frequency of individual coins and banknotes. This is demonstrated in the following table (compare table 11).

Tab. 11 demonstrates alternative spending frequencies of a cash balance of 100 money units (MU). Denomination consists of banknotes with 5, 10, 20, 50, and 100 money units. Spending 100 money units one is able to spend once a – 100 - banknote, twice a 50-bank-note and so on. According to Cassel, frequencies of individual banknotes can be calculated. The individual turnover rate in the first case is equal to one. The 100-banknote can only be spent once to break down the cash balance to zero in a specified economic period. In the second case the turnover rate would also be equal to one. There are two 50-banknotes individually they could be spent once to break down the cash balance to zero in a specified economic period. Without further alternatives it becomes clear that all in table 11 presented denomination alternatives, turnover rates of money are always equal to 'one'. Each individual banknote can only be spent once.

Presented turnover rate of money in tab. 11 is not only the definition according to Cassel but also the definition of the turnover rate of money according to Lutz based on income respectively on cash balance. Since income respectively cash balances can only be spent once in one specified economic period, velocities of money are - according to this definition in equilibrium situations equal to 'one'. Thus, both definitions of turnovers of money lead to the same result.

Furthermore, one recognizes from tab. 11 that the actual problem is not determining turnover rates of money but finding appropriate denominations fitting to incomes respectively cash balances. In non-suitable denominations money supplies are either too large or too small for equilibria income. A further issue is money distribution on individual markets in spatially extended economic areas because assumed timely and spatial point markets hardly exist - or not at all in practice.

Tab. 11: Turnover rates of money in equilibrium situations

income						**100 MU**
denomination 1					1 x 100	100 MU
denomination 2				2 x 50		100 MU
denomination 3			5 x 20			100 MU
denomination 4		10 x 10				100 MU
denomination 5	20 x 5					100 MU
denomination 6		1 x 10	2 x 20	1 x 50		100 MU
denomination 7		3 x 10	1 x 20	1 x 50		100 MU
denomination 8	2 x 5	2 x 10	1 x 20	1 x 50		100 MU
denomination 9	4 x 5	1 x 10	1 x 20	1 x 50		100 MU
denomination 10	10 x 5	5 x 10				100 MU

Source: own presentation

For example an income of 100 MU (denomination) calculates itself (compare denomination 10 in table 11) into a money unit of 10 (number of banknotes) plus 5 (number of banknotes) banknotes of 10 individual notes) plus 5 (number of bank notes) bank notes of 10 (value of individual bank notes) equal to 100 money units.

Presented denominations in tab. 11 are – beyond any doubt – selected simple cases. Every individual banknote is used only once for purchasing in a specified economic period. Finding denominations is more complicated in practice. Denominations do not only depend on equilibria in prices but also on numbers of citizens, numbers of goods, and their prices as well as purchasing- respectively spending behavior of citizens, distributed over a specified economic period. But it is quite certain that turnover rates of money must always be – according to both definitions – equal to 'one'. Thus, the following formal association is valid:

(29) money amount (MU) is equal to sum of individual banknote values (N) times its number

Appropriately, the following contexts of individual banknotes respectively money supplies for turnover of each individual banknote results:

(30) turnover rate of a banknote is equal to one

and

(31) turnover rates of money calculated as sums of turnovers of all banknotes divided by number of banknotes and is equal to 'one'

Turnover rate of money from 15 times 1 divided by 15 is an example for the tenth denomination from Tab. 11.

Assumed for the demonstration in tab. 11 is only cash. The example can even be more complicated introducing deposit- or rather deposit money. In this case deposit money must be subtracted from money supplies determining cash amounts for suitable denominations. Advantage of deposit money has been demonstrated by introducing deposit money. Since deposit money can be denominated at random at predefined money units (coins and banknotes) a denomination cannot be found. Finding denominations would not be at all necessary if monetary systems consisted only of deposit money. Furthermore, a distribution (a transport) of cash to individual regional markets would not be necessary. These are advantages making a monetary system more efficient.

7.3.2 Determining the Turnover Rate of Money in Disequilibrium

Disequilibrium situations distinguish themselves from equilibrium situations not only by making it possible to save and take up credits now but also by observing connections through many specified economic periods and different investment forms as well as capital. Money supplies do not only include cash and deposit money but also amount aggregates referring to investment forms. Considering money amount AM_1, AM_2 and AM_3 (see above) is common practice nowadays.

Now it is possible in a disequilibrium situation to spend more than the income in the actual specified economic period. Assumed is an income of 100 money units (MU) in the current economy period. Additionally, credits of 200 MU are distributed. Thus, money units include 300 MU. Assumed is just a denomination of 100 MU banknotes for the purpose of a simple demonstration. Then there are three possible denomination types of total money supplies: (1) once 100 MU money and 200 MU deposit money, (2) twice 100 MU money and 100 MU deposit money as well as (3) three times 100 MU money and no deposit money at all (compare Tab. 12).

Tab. 12: Turnover rates of money in disequilibrium situations

	Cash	**deposit money**	**money amount**
income			**100 MU**
Credits			**200 MU**
denomination 1	1 x 100	2 x 100	300 MU
denomination 2	2 x 100	1 x 100	300 MU
denomination 3	3 x 100	-	300 MU

Source: own presentation

Turnover of the total money amount is equal to one, because it can only be spent once in the specified economic period. For the denomination of turnover '1' of a 100 MU the turnover is equal to '1'. There is a turnover of '2' for the deposit money because there are two transfers per each individual 100 MU. Both turnover rates have to be added and have to be divided by three, the frequency of the output of the individual banknotes respectively transfer amounts to calculate the turnover rates of money amounts (AM_1) and the deposit amounts (AM_2). Result is again a turnover rate (TR) of one (TR = (1 + 2)/3 = 3/3 = 1). Alternatively, one can also calculate turnover rate of deposit amounts with one, in dividing output 2 rates by 2. Result value for turnover rates of deposit amounts is equal to 'one'. A turnover rate of total money amount (TR_{tAM}) of one is a result by calculating both turnover rates of one and dividing by the turnover rate (two) to be considered ($TR_{tAM} = (AM_1 + AM_2)/2$, $TR_{tAM} = (1 + 1)/2 = 1$).

Thus, it is demonstrated that turnover rates of one banknote, a money component and the complete money amount are equal to 'one'. In other words, there is not any difference demonstrated between the equilibrium- and the disequilibrium situation. However, in the disequilibrium situation there is not only an appropriate denomination of cash amount to be found but also a denomination between cash- and deposit money. Furthermore, cash is to be distributed in the same way on the regional markets as it is distributed at the equilibrium situation.

7.4 There is an amazing Conclusion based on an Equilibrium Model: It also Functions without the Payment Media Money

An amazing conclusion is obtained from the above presented equilibrium model. If wages are also equal to ‘zero’, then one can recognize from tab. 1 that the value related equilibria of individual market participants (companies and citizens) can also be given at the prices of ‘zero’.[25] Only quantity related equilibria have to be created. As consequences from the fact, that value related equilibria can also be possible with prices and wages at ‘zero’. It shows that money is not necessarily seen as payment and store of value. If money is only used as a calculation unit, the national economy functions properly and also optimally. Assumed is proper functioning of a national economy with just using money as a calculation unit to be better than applying money fulfilling the three money functions as means of payment, calculation unit, and store of purchasing power. The national economy respectively economic system is easier and less prone to crisis because there are not any measures necessary against existing insecurities of money values in practice.

Money just used as a calculation unit has been seen as money being secure one hundred percent against systemic crisis! There are three conditions fulfilling the

---

[25] See Cassel, G.: Theoretische Sozialökonomie, 6th ed., Darmstadt 1968 (Leipzig 1918[1]), pp. 121 – 137, esp. pp. 136 f.. Cassel points out: equilibria are determined by relative prices - changed by random multipliers. Hence, prices could also be equal to zero.

security of the currency. If prices are equal to zero, inflation will not be possible. If prices are equal to zero, money will not have any kind of influence. Neutrality of money is given at one hundred percent. If money is just used as a calculation unit, it will be one hundred percent forgery protected. Since all three conditions fulfill the security for the currency at one hundred percent – if money is used as a calculation unit - then money or currency will be one hundred percent safe regarding systemic crisis.

The statement money just being used as a calculation unit to be neutral has coincided with the statement delivered by Wagner. He has discussed money to be neutral whenever it is invisible.[26] Money as calculation units is invisible.

However, advantages of money, prices, and wages have been eliminated by reducing money as a calculation function as well as determining prices and wages equalized to zero. Money stimulation is no longer an approach for achievement. A new, non-monetary performance stimulation instrument must be developed and enforced. For that particular reason cultural- and economic historical behavior patterns of mankind must be reconsidered. Surely, this can only be obtained by long-termed adjustment processes to be initiated on the idea of continuous improvement. For that particular reason, it should be asked for the advantages an economy would benefit from by applying the basis of money with just one function – the calculation unit function.

Contributions to security of currencies, welfare and peace are advantages of such an economy. Since costs for production-, transport-, security-, and transfer of money are omitted, it can be assumed, that an economy based on money with one calculation function to be more efficient than one with traditional money economy. However, functional assumptions for new economic forms are successful applications of non-monetary performance stimulation instruments.

Summarizing, it is old knowledge to just apparently assume money neutrality being in equilibrium (compare Part 3, Paragraph 2). The equilibrium of perfect competition is - in this framework - assumed not to be identical. Assumed is - in this case - a quantity- and value-based equilibrium. Rigid or rather lack of practical conditions are not assumed. However, perfect competition is based on a predominant quantitative equilibrium and rigid conditions.

7.5 How are Macroeconomic Equilibria Created?

Principally, it has already been described above on how economic equilibria[27] are supposed to be created. The methods are to be summarized again.

---

[26] See Wagner, H.-J.: Stabiles oder neutrales Geld ..., p. 79

[27] For equilibria see also Willms, M.: Das Gleichgewichtsproblem in der klassischen und neoklassischen Geldtheorie, in: Jahrbuch für Sozialwissenschaft, Vol. 17 (1966), pp. 166 – 197; Myrdal, G.: Der Gleichgewichtsbegriff als Instrument der geldtheoretischen Analyse, in:

A model of a small insular national economy has demonstrated that economical respectively macro-economic equilibria should be striven for in a "bottom-up-approach" and not in a "top-down-approach". Furthermore, the result has emphasized that economic equilibria consist of two components: a quantity- and a value related one.

First step is to create a quantity related equilibrium based on individual economic production functions or rather appropriate tables for all economic units of a national economy. Appropriate value related equilibria for all economic units should be created by found quantity related equilibria. A value related production function must be taken into account.

If all economic units of a national economy are in a quantity- and value related equilibrium then all partial markets and therefore total markets are at economical (quantity- and value related) equilibria.

Regulation for realizing value related equilibria could be derived from an example of a small insular national economy. This specific regulation is a simple wage-price-rule where each economic subject can be directed individually to. Challenging mathematical knowledge is not necessary at all. In this respect, there is a considerable difference to known equilibrium models in literature, requesting skills in price vector or price-simplex. Additionally, simple wage-price-regulations can be applied without any state interventions (regulation, intervention) taking place. Necessary is only the statutory determination of regulating and training respectively educating for economic entities regarding knowledge and handling of this specified regulation.

7.6 Conclusion

Concluding part six, achieving better theoretic basis for money economies than the combined monetary theory of Keynes and money has become possible. A new approach to the monetary theory results from the detailed consideration of goods markets and creation of quantity- and value related equilibria on goods-, labor- and monetary markets. Thus, a quantity- and value related equilibrium of the total market is also obtained. Thus "real" equilibria have been created on markets and not just identities of a monetary- and goods-economic view of a market economy - as it has been done in the approaches of the quantity- and monetary theory. A "pseudo"-equilibrium as it has been propagated by Keynes with an equilibrium in situations of underemployment is neither created.

The equilibrium approach leads to a further approach of a new monetary theory. Since quantity- and value related equilibria can be created with prices even at 'zero' there is a possibility of a money economy to be created based on money with just one function – the calculation unit function. In this specified economy,

---

Hayek, F.A. (Ed.): Beiträge zur Geldtheorie, Wien 1933 (reprint Berlin a.o. 2007, pp. 361 – 487)

money would be a hundred percent secure to impacts of systemic crisis. In the first new approach of the monetary theory based on real quantity- and value related equilibria, money would only be one hundred percent stable. Since neutrality and counterfeit protection of money are not given, money would not be secure. However, the first approach offers the advantage respecting behavior patterns and thus, is presumably quicker to be realized than the second approach.

Part 7: Estimating the Security of the Euro

The issue raised at the beginning of the book, to answer the security of the euro is to be discussed from two viewpoints: (1) from the viewpoint of the theory and (2) from the viewpoint of the practical policy. Security can be expressed in percentage values. A scale from 'zero' to 'one hundred' percent is presented in fig. 20.

Fig. 20: Scaling the security of the euro

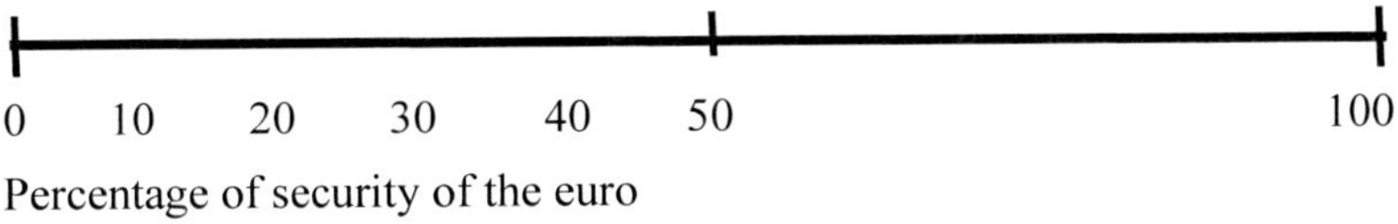

Source: own presentation

If all Euro-States had created a macro-economic equilibrium then, according to the theory, all Euro-States would have created a one hundred percent security of the euro. Requirements of this specified theory would have to be implemented in practice to achieve one hundred percent security of the euro. Three of the demonstrated conditions of the monetary theory would have to be implemented for money security, money stability, neutrality of money, and money counterfeit protection. First, the theory itself would have to be accepted in this new approach, demonstrated in this framework to control the economy respectively accept and make known money supplies. However, it cannot be said, percentage values of theoretical security of the euro in the regime of old (currently predominating) approaches to the control of economy respectively money supplies in the presented fig. 20 because there are no measurement requirements available. It can only be said, that security is currently not at a one hundred percent basis because existing crisis clarify, that there are no macro-economic equilibria in the Euro-States existing.

Estimating euro security from the viewpoint of practical policy is at least as difficult as from the viewpoint of the theory. This statement is also valid that security is currently still under one hundred percent because regulations of the new approach for controlling the economy respectively money supplies has still been unknown and not accepted. Consequently, they can still neither be implemented nor effective.

However, the demonstrated equilibrium model also allows quite a different conclusion, leading to a one hundred percent security of money respectively euro. Since – it has been demonstrated – value related equilibria have also been possible at zero situations with prices and wages. It can be concluded that money is not absolutely necessary creating equilibria in the economy sector. If there is money only available in form of calculation function units in an economy, then insecurity regarding money cannot exist. If there is no money as an exchange-medium and store of purchasing power available, it will additionally be sufficient to create equilibria. Hence one can talk about a "lean-national-economy" situation. This is simple and considerable less complex than the current method of national economic activities.

As has been demonstrated, the euro is secure - on condition stable. Furthermore, it must be neutral and counterfeit proof. These three criteria are to be analyzed separately to be able to judge the current security of the euro.

1. Estimating Euro Stability

Currency stability and – in this case - of the euro, can also determine inflation rates in percent. An inflation rate of 'zero' means that the highest possible stability degree of currencies respectively euro has been achieved. However, an inflation rate of 'one hundred' percent is not the highest possible currency instability, currencies could exhibit. Practice has shown possibilities of considerably higher inflation rates than 'one hundred' percent (i.e. there have been inflation rates in Argentina of over 400 percent about 1980). Since individual persons used to think in a scale from 'zero' to 'one hundred' percent in determining currency stability respectively euro is also a scale applied between 'zero' and 'one hundred' percent.

Fig. 21: Scaling the stability of euro

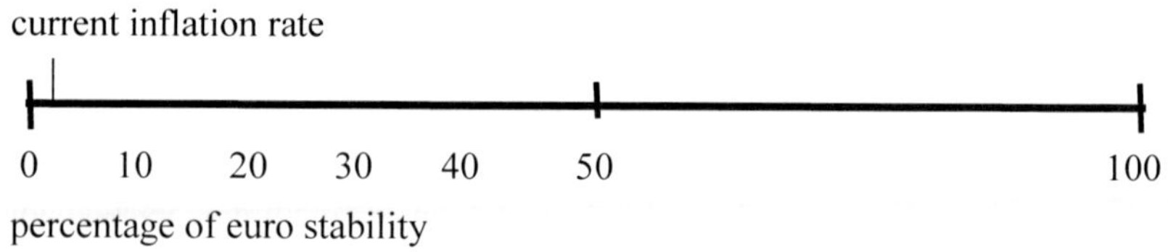

Source: own presentation

Inflation rates for the Federal Republic of Germany have been relatively low in recent years. Inflation rates for the total European Union (EU) respectively member states of the European Money Union (EMU) have been deviating from the Federal Republic of Germany (compare tab. 11). A value of approximately 3 percent has been selected for the graphic presentation of stability of the euro in fig. 21 presented values as upper limit of inflation rates for the assumed period of time. The value has emphasized relatively low inflation rates from the recent past and thus they have reached a relatively high degree of stability for the euro (compare tab. 13).

Tab. 13: Inflation rates for the Republic of Germany, the EU and the EMU 2007 – 2013 (in percent)

Year	inflation rates Federal Republic of Germany	inflation rates EU	inflation rates euro zone (EMU)
2007	2.3	2.3	2.1
2008	2.6	2.7	3.3
2009	0.2	1.0	0.3
2010	1.2	2.1	1.6
2011	2.5	3.1	2.7
2012	2.0	2.6	2.5
2013	1.5	1.5	1.3
2014	-	-	-

Source: Statistisches Bundesamt (Ed.): Statistisches Jahrbuch. Deutschland und Internationales 2014, Wiesbaden 2014, p. 661; Statistisches Bundesamt (Ed.): Statistisches Jahrbuch. Deutschland und Internationales 2013, Wiesbaden 2013, p. 655; Statistisches Bundesamt (Ed.): Statistisches Jahrbuch. Deutschland und Internationales 2012, Wiesbaden 2012, p. 661; Statistisches Bundesamt (Ed.): Statistisches Jahrbuch. Deutschland und Internationales 2011, Wiesbaden 2011, p. 661; Statistisches Bundesamt (Ed.): Statistisches Jahrbuch. Deutschland und Internationales 2010, Wiesbaden 2010, p. 661; Statistisches Bundesamt (Ed.): Statistisches Jahrbuch. Deutschland und Internationales 2009, Wiesbaden 2009, p. 661; Eurostat – Tables, Graphs and Maps Interface (TGM) table (http://ec.europa.eu/ euro-stat/tgm/table.do?tab=table&init=1&language=de&pcode=tec (called upon 06.22.2015))

Values of actual inflation rates are to be set into maximum inflation rates to calculate stability degrees of the euro. If the current inflation was 100%, degree of stability of the currency would be 'one' (100 : 100 = 1). If a base of stability of 'zero' (0 : 100 = 0) was given, then there would be no inflation. The reciprocal value of above calculated values are to be referred to because this particular estimation contradicts usual values. Then the degree of stability at a rate of inflation of 'zero' is equal to 'one' [(100 – 0) : 100 = 1] and at a rate of inflation of 'one hundred' percent equal to 'zero' [(100 – 100) : 100 = 0]. According to this particular calculation method, following inflation rates, represented in table 14 – show the following stability rates (see Tab. 14).

Tab. 14: Stability degrees of the euro for the Federal Republic of Germany, the EU, and the EMU 2007 - 2013

year	stability degree of the euro for the Federal Republic of Germany	stability degree of the euro for the EU	stability degrees of the euro for the euro zone (EMU)
2007	0.977	0.977	0.979
2008	0.974	0.973	0.967
2009	0.998	0.99	0.997
2010	0.988	0.979	0.984
2011	0.975	0.969	0.973
2012	0.98	0.974	0.975
2013	0.985	0.985	0.987
2014	-	-	-

Source: own calculations on the basis of the values of Tab. 13

Since the underlying inflation rates do not represent any accurate values the determined degrees of stability are to be interpreted as estimated values. All inflation rates are not determined of all in a national economy offered goods. This would have been too costly. Therefore a certain number of selected (representative) goods are summarized to a shopping cart and inflation rates are calculated as mean values for these specified shopping carts. Despite simplified calculations of inflation rates, they show suitable estimated values to be considered as appropriate benchmarks. The euro stability degrees for the Federal Republic of Germany in tab. 14 have proven that the EU and the euro zone convey a relatively high euro stability.

2. Estimation of Euro Neutrality

For estimating individual currency neutralities – here the euro – is to form relationships of neutral parts of money supplies of individual currencies to total money supplies. Should 'one hundred' percent of the money amount of a given currency be neutral, the degree of neutrality would be 'one' (100 : 100 = 1) for the specified currency. Corresponding to this a neutrality degree of 'zero' is given if the total money amount is not neutral respectively not any part of money amount is neutral (0 : 100 = 0). Assumed is the neutral portion of 30% in fig. 22. A degree of neutrality of 0.3 respectively 30 percent (30 : 100 = 0.3), has been accounted for between the years 2010 – 2012.

Since, according to Friedman[1] principally just cash is neutral, neutrality degree can be determined by means of calculating the proportion of cash with the total money amount M_3. The respective values for the Federal Republic of Germany and EU have been identified in table 15 for the years 2010 – 2014.

Fig. 22: Scaling neutrality of euro

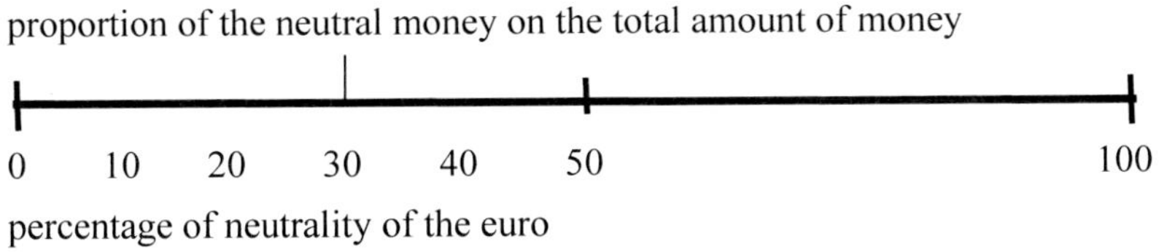

Source: own presentation

Tab. 15: Amount of cash and money M_3 in the Federal Republic of Germany and in the EMU 2010 - 2014 (in Bill. euro)

year	cash in the Federal Republic of Germany	money amount M_3 in the Federal Republic of Germany	cash in the EMU	money amount M_3 in the EMU
2010	200.4	2,082.5	808.6	9,320.8
2011	212.3	2,207.2	857.5	9,535.4
2012	216.3	2,342.6	876.8	9,808.1
2013	226.6	2,319.4	921.2	9,852.8
2014	229.8	2,427.6	980.6	10,317.4

Quelle: Statistisches Bundesamt (Ed.): Statistisches Jahrbuch. Deutschland und Internationales 2014, Wiesbaden 2014, p. 661; Statistisches Bundesamt (Ed.): Statistisches Jahrbuch. Deutschland und Internationales 2013, Wiesbaden 2013, p. 655; Statistisches Bundesamt (Ed.): Statistisches Jahrbuch. Deutschland und Internationales 2012, Wiesbaden 2012, p. 661; Statistisches Bundesamt (Ed.): Statistisches Jahrbuch. Deutschland und Internationales 2011, Wiesbaden 2011, p. 661; Statistisches Bundesamt (Ed.): Statistisches Jahrbuch. Deutschland und Internationales 2010, Wiesbaden 2010, p. 661; Statistisches Bundesamt (Ed.): Statistisches Jahrbuch. Deutschland und Internationales 2009, Wiesbaden 2009, p. 661; Eurostat – Tables, Graphs and Maps Interface (TGM) table (http://ec.europa.eu/ euro-stat/tgm/ table.do?tab=table&init =1&language=de&pcode=tec (called upon 06.22.2015))

Based on presented values in tab. 15 neutrality degrees are shown in tab. 16. Comparing them with stability degrees, they clearly show lower values for neutrality degrees of euros. Values are all below 0.1 or rather 10 percent. Thus, one recognizes that security weaknesses of the euro are positioned at the neutrality degree. Reason is the low portion of cash in the money amount M_3. There has just been a small money amount M_3 having no influence on prices. Consequent-

[1] See part 3, 2. and Friedman, M./Schwartz, A.: Die Definition des Geldes: Nettovermögen und Neutralität als Kriterien …, p. 83

ly, this makes itself noticeable with such a low neutrality degree of the euro (see below).

Tab. 16: Neutrality degrees of euros for the Federal Republic of Germany and the EMU 2010 – 2014

year	degree of neutrality for the Federal Republic of Germany	degree of neutrality of the euro for EMU
2010	0.096230492	0.08675221
2011	0.096185212	0.089928057
2012	0.092333304	0.089395499
2013	0.09769768	0.093496265
2014	0.094661393	0.095043324

Source: own calculations on the basis of the values from tab. 15

3. Estimating Counterfeit Protection of Euro

Estimating currency counterfeit protection – here the euro – is to be determined by means of calculating quotients of parts of forged money supplies and total money supplies. If there is no forged money present then the counterfeit protection degree will be at the highest or equal to 'one'. Calculations are then referred to - as it has been done before - by calculating stability degrees by reciprocal values of proportions of parts of forged money supplies to total supplies [(100 – 0) : 100 = 1]. If total money supplies are forged [(100 – 0) : 100 = 1] then appropriately maximum negative counterfeit protection degrees will be [(100 – 100) : 100 = 0]. Assumed is in fig. 23 the proportion of [(100 – 100): 100 = 0] money of the total money amount of 20 percent. Then the degree of counterfeit protection is 0.8 or rather 80 percent [(100 – 20) : 100 = 0.8].

Fig. 23: Scaling forgery security of the euro

proportion of the forged amount of money

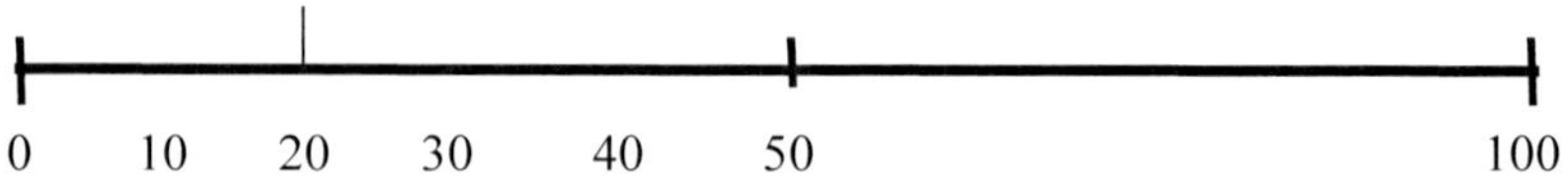

percentage of counterfeit protection of the euro

Source: own presentation

Statistics of the Federal Bureau of Investigation have accounted for registered forged money (compare tab. 17) in the Federal Republic of Germany and euro zone, the European Monetary Union (EMU). The discovered forged money has been specified in banknotes (N) and coins (CO) as well as in unit- and in nominal value.

Tab. 17: Registered forged money in the Federal Republic of Germany and in the EMU (bank notes, N, and coins, CO, according to number and nominal value) 2010 - 2014

year	Federal Republic of Germany		EMU	
	coins	**nominal value**	**coins**	**nominal value**
2010	90,824 67,407	6.7 Mio. euro N 120,000 euro CO	872,535 156,742	51 Mio. euro N 260,000 euro CO
2011	54,427 52,723	6.5 Mio. euro N 90,500 euro CO	667,417 139,380	40 Mio. euro N 90,500 euro CO
2012	59,611 51,988	5.0 Mio. euro N 92,000 euro CO	601,167 118,103	37 Mio. euro N 185,000 euro CO
2013	47,865 52,914	3.8 Mio. euro N 94,000 euro CO	764,536 184,605	51 Mio. euro N 300,000 euro CO
2014	75,631 45,807	5.3 Mio. euro N 81,000 euro CO	1,650,479 473,250	94 Mio. euro N 840,000 euro CO

Source: Bundeskriminalamt (Ed.): Falschgeldkriminalität. Bundeslagebild 2014, Wiesbaden 2014, p. 4 - 7; Bundeskriminalamt (Ed.): Falschgeldkriminalität. Bundeslagebild 2013, Wiesbaden 2013, p. 6 - 10; Bundeskriminalamt (Ed.): Falschgeldkriminalität. Bundeslagebild 2012, Wiesbaden 2012, p. 4 - 7; Bundeskriminalamt (Ed.): Falschgeldkriminalität. Bundeslagebild 2011, Wiesbaden 2011, p. 5 - 9; Bundeskriminalamt (Ed.): Falschgeldkriminalität. Bundeslagebild 2010, Wiesbaden 2010, p. 4 - 9

Shown values in tab. 17 have just been referring to discovered forged money. Dimensions of estimated numbers of undiscovered forged money have not been mentioned in the official statistics and thus must remain open. Even a rough estimation of estimated numbers cannot be achieved. Consequently, it is impossible to calculate accurate degrees of forgery of the euro. Counterfeit protection degree calculations based on discovered forged money just has to serve as a benchmark for counterfeit protection purposes.

Discovered forged money has been set up separately to coins and banknotes respectively, individually according to coins and nominal values set into proportions to total numbers (volumes) of coins respectively banknotes and total values of all coins respectively all banknotes to calculate degrees of forgery. Appropriate values for total numbers and total values are listed for bank notes, and in tab. 19 for coins. Considered are the years 2010 to 2014.

Tab. 18: Volume of bank notes in circulation in the Federal Republic of Germany and in the EMU (according to number of notes and nominal value) between 2010 - 2014

year	Federal Republic Germany notes	nominal value	EMU notes	nominal value
2010	6.8 Mrd. notes	-	14.2 Mrd. notes	839.7 Mrd. euro
2011	6.8 Mrd. notes	-	14.9 Mrd. notes	888.6 Mrd. euro
2012	6.8 Mrd. notes	-	15.7 Mrd. notes	912.6 Mrd. euro
2013	6.8 Mrd. notes	-	16.5 Mrd. notes	956.2 Mrd. euro
2014	6.8 Mrd. notes	-	17.5 Mrd. notes	1,016. 5 Mrd. euro

Source: Bundeskriminalamt (Ed.): Falschgeldkriminalität. Bundeslagebild 2014, Wiesbaden 2014, p. 8; Bundeskriminalamt (Ed.): Falschgeldkriminalität. Bundeslagebild 2013, Wiesbaden 2013, p. 10; Bundeskriminalamt (Ed.): Falschgeldkriminalität. Bundeslagebild 2012, Wiesbaden 2012, p. 7; Bundeskriminalamt (Ed.): Falschgeldkriminalität. Bundeslagebild 2011, Wiesbaden 2011,p. 10; Bundeskriminalamt (Ed.): Falschgeldkriminalität. Bundeslagebild 2010, Wiesbaden 2010, p. 10; Europäische Zentralbank: Jahresbericht 2014, Frankfurt am Main 2015, p. 85; Europäische Zentralbank: Jahresbericht 2013, Frankfurt am Main 2014, p. 108; Europäische Zentralbank: Jahresbericht 2012, Frankfurt am Main 2013, p. 103; Europäische Zentralbank: Jahresbericht 2011, Frankfurt am Main 2012, p. 102; Europäische Zentralbank: Jahresbericht 2010, Frankfurt am Main 2011, p. 121

Tab. 19: Volume of coins in circulation in the Federal Republic of Germany and in the EMU (according to number of coins and nominal value) between 2010 - 2014

year	Federal Republic of Germany		EMU	
	number of coins	nominal value	number of coins	nominal value
2010	-	-	92.9 Mrd. coins	22.3 Mrd. euro
2011	-	-	97.8 Mrd. coins	23.1 Mrd. euro
2012	-	-	102.0 Mrd. coins	23.7 Mrd. euro
2013	-	-	106.0 Mrd. coins	24.2 Mrd. euro
2014	-	-	110.9 Mrd. coins	25.0 Mrd. euro

Source: Europäische Zentralbank: Jahresbericht 2014, Frankfurt am Main 2015, p. 85; Europäische Zentralbank: Jahresbericht 2014, Frankfurt am Main 2015, p. 85; Europäische Zentralbank: Jahresbericht 2013, Frankfurt am Main 2014, p. 109; Europäische Zentralbank: Jahresbericht 2012, Frankfurt am Main 2013, p. 104; Europäische Zentralbank: Jahresbericht 2011, Frankfurt am Main 2012, p. 103; Europäische Zentralbank: Jahresbericht 2010, Frankfurt am Main 2011, p. 121

Tab. 20: Degrees of forgery security of the euro bank notes for the Federal Republic of Germany and in the EMU (according to number of coins) between 2010 – 2014

year	degree of forgery of the euro bank notes for the Federal Republic of Germany	degree of forgery of the euro bank notes for the EMU
2010	0.999986644	0.999938553
2011	0.999991997	0.999955206
2012	0.999991234	0.999961709
2013	0.999992962	0.999953664
2014	0.999988878	0.999905686

Source: own calculations based on values from tab. 17, and 18

Since money volumes in circulation have only been accounted for in coins and not in its nominal value because nominal values are, according to the Federal Bureau of Investigation "just conditionally ….. resilient"[2] (comp. Tab. 18), the counterfeit protection degree of the euro for the Federal Republic of Germany

[2] Bundeskriminalamt (Ed.): Falschgeldkriminalität. Bundeslagebild 2014, Wiesbaden 2014, p. 7

can only be referred to as coin units in table 20. Additionally, presentation of banknotes must be limited to the Federal Republic of Germany. Appropriate coin values cannot be calculated because of missing indications in the statistics of the Federal Bureau of Investigation. Furthermore, values for the European Union cannot be determined for the European Union but just for the euro zone (compare tab. 20).

Since the above presented calculation cannot be based on money volumes, calculating counterfeit protection degrees (compare tab. 17 and 18) are achieved by dividing registered banknotes according to units by circulating banknotes. Thus, a relatively high counterfeit protection degree of the euro has been registered in the Federal Republic of Germany and euro zone from 2010 to 2014. Values have just been under 'one' respectively 100 percent and thus have almost reached optimum values of counterfeit protection security. However, it should be noted that values have just been considered as values with registered counterfeited banknotes; actual numbers of counterfeit banknotes still remain open.

In tab. 21 counterfeit protection security degrees of euros for euro banknotes in the EMU referring to nominal values for the years 2010 to 2014 have been listed.

Tab. 21: Degrees of forgery security of euro banknotes for the Federal Republic of Germany and the EMU (with regard to the nominal value) 2010 – 2014

year	**degree of forgery of the euro bank notes for the Federal Republic of Germany**	**degree of forgery of the euro bank notes for the EMU**
2010	-	0.999939264
2011	-	0.999954985
2012	-	0.999959456
2013	-	0.9999466663
2014	-	0.999907525

Source: own calculations on the basis of the values from the tab. and 18

From tab. 21 can be observed that the counterfeit degree of banknotes regarding nominal values is at a low level. Accordingly, a high counterfeit protection security degree of the euro located above 0.99 or rather 99.9 percent and has almost reached the ideal value from one or rather 100 percent.

Tab. 22: Degrees of forgery security of the euro bank coins for the Federal Republic of Germany and the EMU (referring to numbers) 2010 – 2014

year	degree of forgery of the euro bank coins for the Federal Republic of Germany	degree of forgery of the euro bank coins for the EMU
2010	-	0.999998312
2011	-	0.999998574
2012	-	0.999998842
2013	-	0.999998258
2014	-	0.999995732

Source: own calculations based on values from Tab. 17 and 19

Counterfeit protection security degrees of the euros for coins is listed in tab. 22. Based on coins counterfeit protection security degrees for euro coins in the EMU the value has also been 0.99 or rather 99.9 percent.

Finally counterfeit protection security degrees for euro coins listed in tab. 23 regarding the nominal value. This value is also above the EMU 0.99 respectively 99.9 percent.

Tab. 23: Degrees of forgery security of euro bank coins for the Federal Republic of Germany and EMU (regarding nominal numbers) 2010 – 2014

year	degree of forgery of the euro bank coins for the Federal Republic of Germany	degree of forgery of the euro bank coins for the EMU
2010	-	0.99998834
2011	-	0.999991342
2012	-	0.999992194
2013	-	0.999987603
2014	-	0.9999664

Source: own calculations on the basis of the values from Tab. 17 and 19

It is therefore certain that euros regarding the banknotes and coins in each individual case has had - according to unit and nominal value a high counterfeit protection security degree. Values could only be calculated predominantly for the euro zone, the EMU. High similarity of counterfeit protection security degrees demonstrated in tab. 20 for the Federal Republic of Germany and the EMU allow the conclusion that regarding the other features – it does not show any values in the statistics - there is a high similarity. One can say the euro has been signified, regarding to the listed features for the EMU as well as for the Federal Republic of Germany by a high counterfeit protection security degree.

4. Estimation of Risk Potential of Current Security Standard of Euro

The degree of currency security – here the euro – is achieved by adding stability-, neutrality-, and counterfeit protection security degrees. Values attained by adding should be divided by the number of values (here 3) to calculate degrees of security in scaling ranges of three initial values. Assumed is an example with the degree of stability of 0.3, a degree of neutrality of 0.5, a counterfeit protection security degree of 0.1. A degree of security of 0.3 ((0, 3 + 0, 5 + 0, 1)/3 = 0, 9: 3 = 0, 3) is then given. Multiplying this result with 100 percent will result with a percentage value of 30 percent (compare Fig. 24).

Calculated values for the degree of security of the euro are presented in table 24. The values of the Federal Republic of Germany and the EMU are listed. However, degrees of security have not been calculated for all features. Based on high similarities by different features achieved by other calculated degrees, just the degree of security for the euro banknotes regarding units for the Federal Republic of Germany and the EMU for the years 2010 to 2013 (compare tab. 24) were calculated. Since the inflation rates for the year 2014 had not been asserted with absolute certainty (only predicted values) in the official statistics of the year 2014, the values for the year 2014 were not calculated. Consequently, a stability degree was not calculated in the year 2014.

Fig. 24: Scaling classification/ranking of the euro

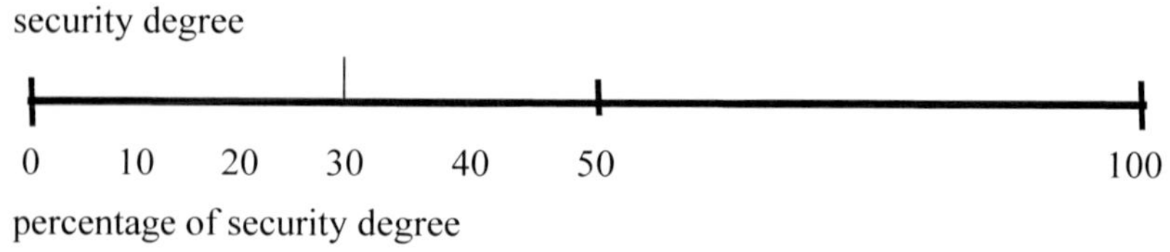

Source: own presentation

Tab. 24: Security degree of the euro for Federal Republic of Germany and the EMU (regarding euro banknotes and coin units) 2012 - 2014

year	security degree of the euro for the Federal Republic of Germany	security degree of the euro for the EMU
2010	(0.988 + 0.096230492 + 0.999986644)/3 = 0.69474	(0.984 + 0.08675221 + 0.999938553)/3 = 0.690230254
2011	(0.975 + 0.096185212 + 0.999991997)/3 = 0.69039	(0.973 + 0.089928057 +)/3 0.999955206 = 0.687627754
2012	(0.98 + 0.092333304 + 0.999991234)/3 = 0.6907748	(0.975 + 0.089395499 + 0.999961709)/3 = 0.688119069
2013	(0.985 + 0.09769768 + 0.999992962)/3 = 0.694230214	(0.987 + 0.093496265 + 0.999953664)/3 = 0.693344301
2014	-	-

Source: own calculations based on values from tab.12, 14, and 18

Security degrees obtained for the euro (compare tab. 24) reflect an estimation based on actual values from official statistics. It is concerned with a current estimation. It does not represent an estimation of future developments of euro security. An estimation of euro security must be observed by existing hazard potentials for the next years. The hazard potentials have been caused – above all - by high national debts of some EMU and EU member states, by general economic developments as well as small neutral money supplies.[3] Generally, the statement is valid, every crisis whether caused systemically- or externally means a hazard potential for the security of the euro.

Listed security degrees for the euro are clearly seen under calculated stability degrees and counterfeit protection security degrees. Relative low neutrality degrees obtained by low cash portions M_3 (see above and annex 4, fig. 27) are specified reasons for that.

Principally, the general statement is valid, a hundred percent security is impossible. This statement is to be applied analogue to the euro. However, it is possible to protect the euro a hundred percent against systemic crisis. It is just impacts caused by external crisis exerted on the euro giving no protection. Protection of the euro against systemic crisis is – as it has been demonstrated in part 6, paragraph 7.4 – achieved, whenever it has just been used as a calculation unit and not as a payment- and a store of value means as well. Prices must then be

[3] See Annex 4, Fig. 27

equal to 'zero'. Since there is no influence on prices occurring, the euro is neutral. In other words, stability for the euro has been achieved. Since there has been no money circulated – secure not to be forged, it is neutral. Three conditions adhere to currency security – here of the euro. Furthermore, economy is in equilibrium. Systemic crisis are impossible in equilibrium situations.

However, whether or not a particular "ideal situation" will ever be reached - remains an issue. Every individual person must be ready to change his behavior and the structure of economy fundamentally. These particular changes should be striven for sustainable prosperity and peace. Realization of these objectives justifies these specified changes!

Part 8: Consequences for Politics

Explanations to the security of the euro are to be summarized in a short form and consequences for policy, especially for economic policies as well as deducing monetary- and currency policies.

Based on these explanations is the very old quotation by Wicksell that one unifying European currency would secure peace. This specified current valid explanation cannot be stressed strongly enough.

Folks have been referring to the euro as "teuro". Furthermore, it has also been demonstrated to be an "accelerator". The euro leads more readily to crisis. One of the reasons is the store of value function of money. In contrast to the calculation unit- and payment media function of money – both have remained unaffected by the euro introduction – the store of value function has been influenced by exchange rate dependency to the former currency. Individuals still continue to reflect on value ratios as they had been used to with the former currency.

Emphasis today is on "euro-crisis". Whether this is adequate or not, should remain an issue. However, it is certain that for current crisis additional causes have occurred changing value ratios by the new currency – the euro. Discussed are different rescue measures for securing the euro. All measures cannot be generally ranked as not functioning at an optimum because the supported conditions have not been complied to. Money has to be neutral – this fact is to be especially mentioned. This specified condition has just not been playing a role in monetary- and currency policy. This can be clearly observed by the many suggestions rescuing the euro – instead of striving for neutrality, creating more non neutral money is the objective.

Since market equilibria and full harmonization of the member states have not been striven for, convergence criteria and stability- and growth pacts including additional Six-Pack cannot secure the euro.

The proven conditions of monetary- and currency theories for monetary securities have been discussed for many years. Three conditions include stability, neutrality, and counterfeit protection. The money amount control concept had been additionally discussed. Methods had been presented to realize these specified conditions.

Summarized could be said that it is possible to improve the money amount control and therefore the stability of the euro. It is more difficult to enforce neutrality and counterfeit protection. However, it is actually possible two achieve both conditions. However, the measures are controversial and are against traditional system structures and behaviors.

Applying money, just as one calculation unit, would be an extreme possibility guaranteeing all three conditions for security of a currency simultaneously. This specified solution would be a more radical revolution of monetary policies than monetarism would have brought about.

Actually, the idea is not topical and also not impractical. However, it is not to be achieved at a short time. It violates current "walls in minds" to be overcome hopefully, after a not too long a process to overcome "tough" learn- and experience processes.

1. Euro Relatively Secure

Evaluation of all official statistics has demonstrated relative secure states of the euro based on current relatively low inflation and low registration of forged euro-money supplies. However, neutrality is relatively low.

Degree of security of the euro has been at approximately 0.6 (or rather 60 percent) up to 0.7 (or rather 70 percent) in the observed years. Measured values are at a scale from zero to one (or rather 0 and 100 percent).

2. Security can still be Improved

Security of the euro can still be improved by increasing money amount controls and thereby increasing stability.

Increasing security of the euro, additionally to increasing neutrality and counterfeit protection are theoretically possible - but currently not to be enforced.

3. Absolute Security Impossible

Theoretical possibility of high graded security of the euro is – as it has been said before – currently not to be achieved. Therefore, the following applies also to the security of the euro - no absolute security is possible. Currently, in the monetary- and currency system, there has always been a possibility and will always be a hazard potential, considerably influencing high security. Internal hazard potentials on the euro result from small cash portions of money supplies. By far, the larger share of money amounts have not been neutral and therefore it can be influenced by an inflation.

4. Hazard Potential Externally of Monetary System

The hazard potential for the security of the euro is located for the biggest part externally of the monetary- and currency systems. Above all, three facts can cause a security risk. Included is the missing full harmonization of economic structures and – regulation in the euro -, but also in EU member states, high national debts, and high subsidy payments.

4.1 No Complete Harmonization

Harmonization as a functional prerequisite for integrating communities has already been recognized and considered at formulating contracts in Rome. At that particular time an extendable and harmonizing time (transitional time) to be shortened (flexible) by twelve years was agreed upon by the old six founding states.[1] This specified time already expired in the year 1969 without enforcing a full harmonization respectively a common market. Also the Action for the Failure to Act in the year 1983[2], regarding full harmonization was not able to achieve anything positive.

Achieved harmonization essentially, refers rather to social and technical sectors. Harmonization in important economic sectors has hardly been enforced. Above all taxes, prices, and wages have not been fully harmonized. However, policy success has always been celebrated with extensions of communities. But they have overlooked that each individual acceptance of a state has caused additional harmonization requests with increasing numbers of member states not making harmonization any easier at all.

As laid down, functionality in integration communities, full harmonization has become more and more imperative. Especially, same prices in member states without achieving equal wages have been causing undesired "mass immigration" or rather "wage tourism" from east to west and south to north. These migrations and the undesired side effects can only be stopped by achieving full harmonization.

For that particular reason it is an important requirement to politicians to enforce full harmonization once and for all, or else guaranteed existence of the European Union is impossible.

4.2 High Level of National Debt

A hazard potential of the euro should not be underestimated based on high national debts in many member states. High national debts do not remain without any impacts on monetary- and currency policies. On the other hand, national debts can only be avoided by adjusting monetary policies. National debts have been seen on many occasions as problems. The current national debt crisis in Greece clearly has demonstrated the difficulties a nation and a monetary system can come up with.

Reality has been demonstrating that national debts have steadily been increasing and cannot be reduced by "normal" methods. This practical knowledge can be

[1] See Vertrag zur Gründung der Europäischen Wirtschaftsgemeinschaft vom 25. März 1957 (BGBL. II 1957, p. 766), Art. 8

[2] See Gerichtshof der Europäischen Gemeinschaften: Das Europäische Parlament gegen den Rat der Europäischen Gemeinschaft (Klageschrift), Reg.-No. 171124, Luxemburg 1983

theoretically supported by a simple equilibrium model. Consequence is requesting to prohibit national debts for all member states in the European Union.

4.3 High Levels of Subsidies

High national debts in many member states of the European Union have been caused by high subsidy payments for securing market functionality. Subsidies are partly paid on the amount- as well as on the demand side. However, necessity of subsidies is not necessarily justified but rather demonstrated as superfluous. High subsidies have, above all two serious disadvantages: (1) they falsify behavior of economic units on markets and (2) lead to high national debts.

Since national debts have been caused by the above mentioned disadvantages and their prohibition has been called for, it is just a consequence to request prohibition of subsidies for all of member states of the European Union.

5. Peace - Most Important Factor

Summarizing, it is of a high importance to discuss the knowledge of Wicksell proposing a mutual European currency to secure peace. If that is the case then there must be a unified global currency requested. However, that is "dreams" for the future. Currently is important to secure a unified European currency and therefore to secure the European Union.

This demand has a simple and important reason: without spending peace, all civilian goods will not have the desired benefit and lose their value! Whoever accepts this knowledge and wants to create peace must create and maintain the functional conditions for a uniform currency and an integration community – such as the European Union.

Annexes

Annex 1: Introduction of euro into the EMU-Member States

(situation May 2015, 19 EMU-Member States)
The euro was introduced as a book currency on the 1.1.1999 and was introduced as cash in the following countries as the official currency on the 1.1.2002: France, Italy, Germany, Belgium, the Netherlands, Luxembourg, Austria, Finnland, Spain, Portugal, and Ireland (all 1999), Greece (2001), Slowenia (2007), Cypress, Malta (2008), Estonia (2011), Latvia, Lithuania (2015).
The following 9 EU-Member States have not yet introduced the euro:
Great Britain, Denmark, Sweden, Poland, Bulgaria, Romania, CSSR, Hungary, and Croatia.

Annex 2: Development of the Velocity of Money

Tab. 25: Values for the Gross National Product (GNP) and the amount of money $M_1 - M_3$ for the Federal Republic of Germany 1997 - 2014 (in Bill. of euro)

year	GNP	money amount M_1	money amount M_2	money amount M_3
1997	1,964.65	465.0	1,167.8	1,212.7
1998	2,015.25	513.4	1,258.2	1,302.1
1999	2,061.81	557.6	1,321.6	1,395.3
2000	2,113.50	574.6	1,309.4	1,381.2
2001	2,176.81	601.6	1,367.0	1,466.9
2002	2,206.28	583.5	1,349.2	1,457.1
2003	2,217.05	631.9	1,395.2	1,506.0
2004	2,267.58	655.4	1,423.3	1,518.6
2005	2,297.82	725.8	1,490.1	1,593.6
2006	2,390.20	760.0	1,568.7	1,673.6
2007	2,510.11	789.7	1,737.4	1,857.2
2008	2,558.02	832.8	1,883.0	2,034.9
2009	2,456.66	1,015.9	1,865.7	1,994.9
2010	2,576.22	1,106.7	1,944.6	2,082.5
2011	2,699.10	1,170.4	2,072.8	2,207.2
2012	2,749.90	1,365.7	2,231.6	2,342.6
2013	2,809.48	1,448.1	2,293.9	2,319.4
2014	2,903.79	1,557.8	2,402.1	2,426.5

Quelle: Statistisches Bundesamt (Ed.): Volkswirtschaftliche Gesamtrechnungen. Bruttoinlandsprodukt ab 1970. Vierteljahres- und Jahresergebnisse. 1. Vierteljahr 2015, Wiesbaden 2015, o. Seitenangabe; http:/www.sachverständigenrat-wirtschaft.de/zr_deutschland.html (called upon 08.03.2015)

Tab. 26: Velocity (V) of money in the Federal Republic of Germany 1997 - 2014

year	V (M_1)	V (M_2)	V (M_3)
1997	4.2505376	1.68235143	1.62006267
1998	3.92530191	1.60169289	1.54769219
1999	3.69765065	1.56008626	1.47768222
2000	3.67821093	1.61409806	1.53019114
2001	3.61836769	1.59239941	1.48395255
2002	3.78111397	1.63525052	1.51415826
2003	3.50854566	1.58905533	1.47214475
2004	3.45984132	1.59318485	1.49320427
2005	3.16591347	1.54205758	1.44190512
2006	3.14500000	1.52368203	1.42817878
2007	3.17856148	1.44475078	1.35155611
2008	3.07158982	1.35848115	1.25707406
2009	2.41821045	1.31674975	1.23147025
2010	2.32783952	1.32480716	1.23708043
2011	2.30613465	1.30215168	1.22286154
2012	2.01354617	1.23225488	1.17386664
2013	1.94011463	1.22476132	1.21129602
2014	1.86403261	1.20885475	1.19669895

Source: own calculations on the basis of Tab. 25

Fig. 25: Velocity (V) of the money in the Federal Republic of Germany 1997 - 2014

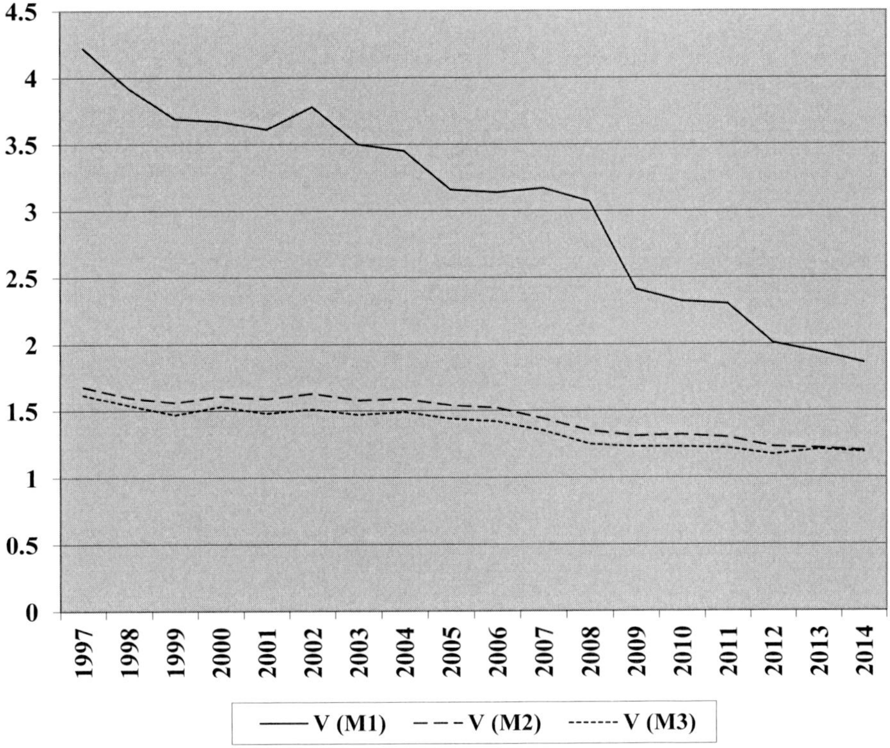

Source: Tab. 26

Tab 27: Values for the Gross National Product (GNP) and money supplies M_1 – M_3 for the euro zone (EMU) 1997 - 2014 (in Bill. euro)

year	GNP	money amount M_1	money amount M_2	money amount M_3
1997	6,132.938	1,626.9	3,687.1	4,265.5
1998	6,379.245	1,785.4	3,920.1	4,471.1
1999	6,674.011	1,972.0	4,142.3	4,708.9
2000	7,029.969	2,084.6	4,299.6	4,910.3
2001	7,351.953	2,279.0	4,684.4	5,446.7
2002	7,604.891	2,499.4	4,981.4	5,807.8
2003	7,825.016	2,727.1	5,298.0	6,180.9
2004	8,156.695	2,948.9	5,632.3	6,568.2
2005	8,451.320	3.482.1	6,168.7	7,130.7
2006	8,894.994	3,758.6	6,743.8	7,802.0
2007	9,392.907	3,901.3	7,436.9	8,691.9
2008	9,627.011	4,035.7	8,103.1	9,423.9
2009	9,284.439	4,556.2	8,275.1	9,381.5
2010	9,540.129	4,754.4	8,472.3	9,320.9
2011	9,799.480	4,866.6	8,671.2	9,535.4
2012	9,845.574	5,168.7	9,045.7	9,809.1
2013	9,930.601	5,444.5	9,249.4	9,852.3
2014	10,110.858	5,956.5	9,682.9	10,315.5

Source: http:/ec.europa.eu/eurostat/statistics-explained/index.php/National_accounts_GDP (called upon 08.03.2015); http:/www.sachverständigenrat-wirtschaft.de/zr_deutschland.html (called upon 08.03.2015)

Tab. 28: Velocity (V) of money for the euro zone (EMU) 1997 - 2014

year	V (M_1)	V (M_2)	V (M_3)
1997	3.769708034	1.663350056	1.437800492
1998	3.573006049	1.627316905	1.426773054
1999	3.384386917	1.611184849	1.417318482
2000	3.37233474	1.635028607	1.431678105
2001	3.225955682	1.569454573	1.349799512
2002	3.042686645	1.526657365	1.30942715
2003	2.869354259	1.476975462	1.26599945
2004	2.766012751	1.44819967	1.24184632
2005	2.427075615	1.370032584	1.185202014
2006	2.366571064	1.318988404	1.140091515
2007	2.407635147	1.263013756	1.080650606
2008	2.385462497	1.188065185	1.021552754
2009	2.037759317	1.121973028	0.989653999
2010	2.006589475	1.126037676	1.023520154
2011	2.013619365	1.130118092	1.027694696
2012	1.904845319	1.088425882	1.003718384
2013	1.823969327	1.073648129	1.007947484
2014	1.697449509	1.044197296	0.980161698

Source: own calculations on the basis of tab. 27

Fig 26: Velocity (V) of the money for the euro zone (EMU) 1997 - 2014

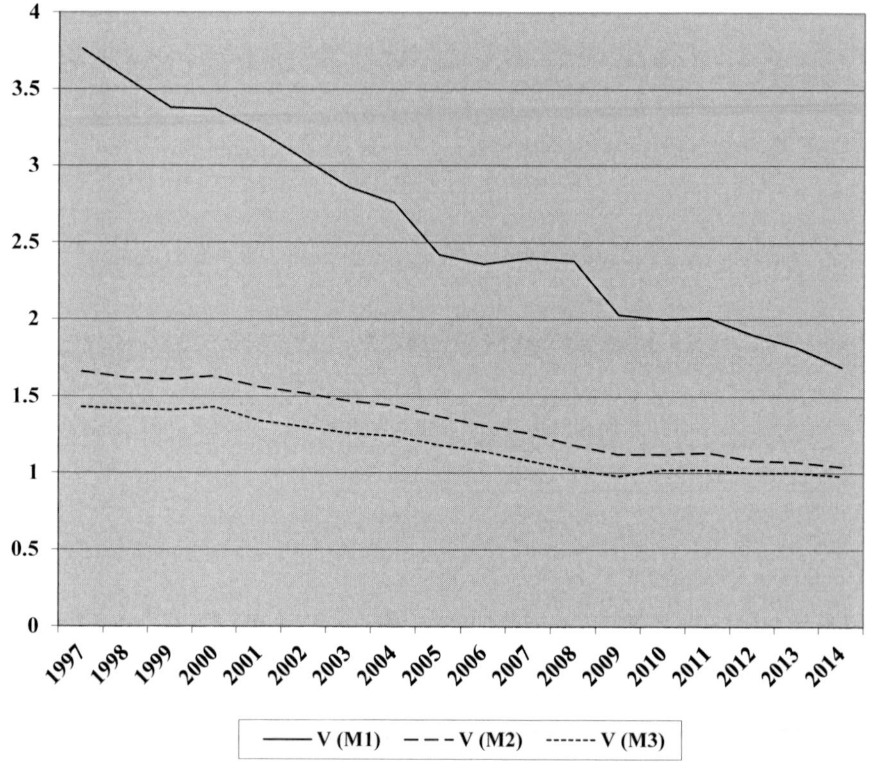

Source: Tab. 2

Annex 3: Development of inflation in the Federal Republic of Germany

Tab. 29: Inflation rates (consumer prices) for euro zone (EMU) 1997 – 2014

year	inflation rate (%)	year	inflation rate (%)
1950	- 6.4	1983	3.2
1951	7.6	1984	2.5
1952	2.1	1985	2.0
1953	- 1.7	1986	- 0.1
1954	0.4	1987	0.2
1955	1.4	1988	1.2
1956	2.8	1989	2.8
1957	2.0	1990	2.6
1958	2.3	1991	3.7
1959	0.6	1992	5.1
1960	1.6	1993	4.5
1961	2.5	1994	2.6
1962	2.8	1995	1.8
1963	3.0	1996	1.4
1964	2.4	1997	2.0
1965	3.2	1998	1.0
1966	3.3	1999	0.6
1967	1.9	2000	1.4
1968	1.6	2001	2.0
1969	1.8	2002	1.4
1970	3.6	2003	1.1
1971	5.2	2004	1.6
1972	5.4	2005	1.6
1973	7.1	2006	1.5
1974	6.9	2007	2.3
1975	6.0	2008	2.6
1976	4.2	2009	0.3
1977	3.7	2010	1.1
1978	2.7	2011	2.1
1979	4.1	2012	2.0
1980	5.4	2013	1.5
1981	6.3	2014	0.9
1982	5.2	-	-

Source: Statistisches Bundesamt (Ed.): Preise. Verbraucherpreisindizes für Deutschland. Lange Reihen ab 1948, Wiesbaden 2015, p. 4 – 5; the values for years 1950 to 1961, 1962 to 1991 and 1992 to 2014 are not directly comparable because of breaks in the time rows.

Annex 4: Graphic presentation of internal risk potential of the security of the euro

Fig. 27: Proportions of the neutral cash amount and the non neutral money supply on total money amount M_3 in EMU in the year 2014 (in %)

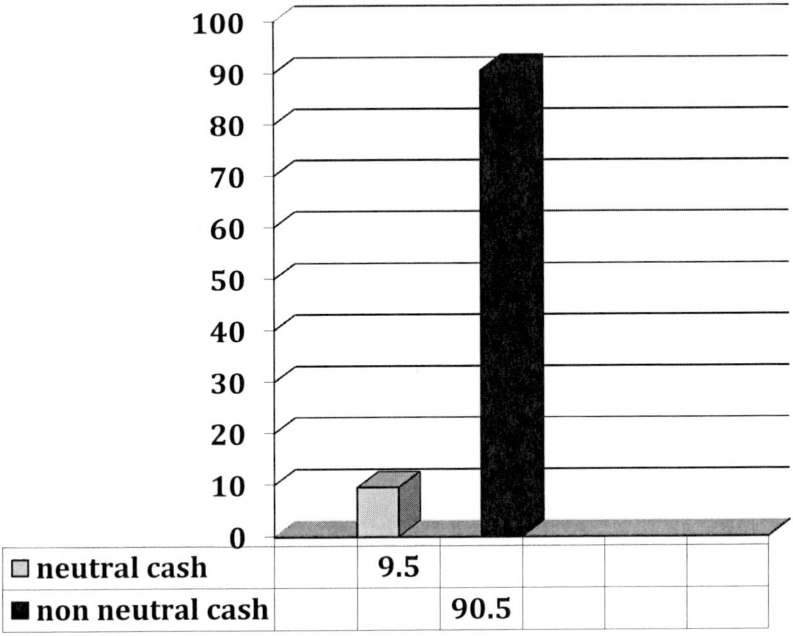

Source: own calculations according to http:/www.sachverständigenrat-wirtschaft.de/zr_deutschland.html (called upon 08.03.2015)

Annex 5: Formulas

2.1 Fisher Equation of Exchange:

(32) $AM \bullet V = T \bullet P$

with

AM = amount of money

V = velocity of money

T = exchange volume

P = price level

2.2 Variants of the Fisher Equation of Exchange

(33) $AM \bullet V = Y \bullet P$

with

AM = amount of money

V = velocity of money

Y = national income

P = price level

(34) $AM \bullet V = GNP \bullet P$

with

AM = amount of money

V = velocity of money

GNP = gross national product

P = price level

(35) $AM \bullet V = GDP \bullet P$

with

AM = amount of money

V = velocity of money

GDP = gross domestic product

P = price level

For each individual variant of the Fisher Equation of Exchange is an additional formulation possible – in applying cash coefficients instead of the velocities of money:

(36) $V = 1 / cc$

with

V = velocity of money

cc = cash coefficient

2.3 Formulating the market equilibria in the approach of Keynes:

Goods market equilibrium

(37) S (Y) = I (i)

with

S = anticipated savings (goods on offer)

Y = national income

I = anticipated investments (goods demand)

i = interest rate

Money market equilibrium

(38) AM = PLI (Y, i)

with

M = amount of money (money supply)

P = price level } money demand

LI = demand for real balances (liquidity)

Y = national income

i = interest rate

Labor market equilibrium

(39) L^n (w/P, Y) + L^u = L^a (w/P)

with

L^n = demand for labor

w = nominal wages

P = price level

Y = national income

L^u = unemployment (underemployment)

L^a = labor supply (job offers)

Macroeconomic production function to calculate the demand for labor

(40) Y = f (L^n)

with

Y = national income

L^n = demand for labor

f = function of …

2.4 Formulating the market equilibria in the new approach of monetary theory

Value related production function for enterprise X

(41) $R = f(C)$

with

R = revenue

C = costs

(42) $R = f(LC + CAC)$

with

R = revenue

LC = costs of engaged work

CAC = costs of engaged capital

Value related macroeconomic production function

$$(43)\quad Y = f\left(\sum_{t=1}^{T} LC_t + \sum_{t=1}^{T} CAC_t\right)$$

with

Y = national income (gross national product, gross domestic product)

LC_t = costs of engaged work for transaction t

CAC_t = costs of engaged capital for transaction t

t = index of transactions, t = 1, …, T

goods market equilibrium

quantity related equilibrium

(44) $GQ^o = GQ^d$

with

GQ^o = quantity of goods offered

GQ^d = quantity of goods demanded

Value-based equilibrium for enterprise X

(45) $R = LC + CAC$

with

R = revenue

LC = costs of engaged work

CAC = costs of engaged capital

C = sum LC + CAC

Equilibrium conditions

(46) $GQ^d/NE = GQ^o/NE$

with

GQ^o = quanitity of goods offered

GQ^d = quantity of goods demanded

NE = number of employees (citizens)

(47) w/NE = EXP/NE

with

w = wage

EXP = expenses

NE = number of employees (citizens)

(48) Σ QUoG = Σ NE

with

QUoG = quantity units of offered goods

NE = number of employees (citizens)

(49) p/QUoG = w/NE

with

p = price of offered goods

QUoG = quantity units of offered goods

w = wage

NE = number of employees (citizens)

Money market equilibrium

(50) AM = p/QUoG

with

AM = amount of money (money supply)

p = price of good } money demand

QUoG = quantity unit of goods

(51) AM = R

with

AM = amount of money

R = revenue of enterprise X

(52) $AM = \sum_{j=1}^{J} w_j$

with

AM = amount of money

w_j = wage of employee j

j = index of employees (citizens), j = 1, …, J

(53) AM = w/NE • AZMA

with

AM = amount of money

w = wage

NE = number of employees (citizens)

AZMA = Anzahl der Mitarbeiter (Bürger)

Arbeitsmarktgleichgewicht

(54) NoJ = NoC

with

NoJ = number of jobs

NoC = number of citizens

(55) w/NE = p/QUoG

with

w = wage

NE = number of employees (citizens)

p = price of good

QUoG = quantity unit of good

Turnover rate in equlibrium

(56) $TR_{Note\ \mathbf{n}} = 1$

with

TR = turnover rate of individual bank notes or amount of money

n = index of bank notes, n = 1, …, N

(57) $TR_{am} = (TR_{note1} + \ldots + TR_{noteN})/N$

with

TR = turnover rate of individual bank notes or amount of money

n = index of bank notes, n = 1, …, N

Literature

Bekanntmachung über das Inkrafttreten des Vertrags zur Einrichtung des Europäischen Stabilitätsmechanismus (ESM) vom 1. Oktober 2012 (BGBl. II, S. 1086)

Bernholz, P.: Currency Competition. Inflation, Gresham's Law and Exchange Rate, in: Zeitschrift für die gesamte Staatswissenschaft, Vol. 145 (1989), pp. 465 – 488

Bris, A./Koskinen, Y./Nilson, M.: The Euro and Corporate Valuations, in: The Review of Financial Studies, Vol. 22 (2009), pp. 3171 - 3209

Brunner, K./Meltzer, A.H.: Die Verwendung von Geld: Geld in der Theorie einer Tauschwirtschaft, in: Brunner, K./Monissen, H.G./Neumann, M.J.M (Ed.): Geldtheorie, Köln 1974, pp. 50 – 73

Bundeskriminalamt (Ed.): Falschgeldkriminalität. Bundeslagebild 2010, Wiesbaden 2010

Bundeskriminalamt (Ed.): Falschgeldkriminalität. Bundeslagebild 2011, Wiesbaden 2011

Bundeskriminalamt (Ed.): Falschgeldkriminalität. Bundeslagebild 2012, Wiesbaden 2012

Bundeskriminalamt (Ed.): Falschgeldkriminalität. Bundeslagebild 2013, Wiesbaden 2013

Bundeskriminalamt (Ed.): Falschgeldkriminalität. Bundeslagebild 2014, Wiesbaden 2014

Cassel, G.: Theoretische Sozialökonomie, 6th ed., Darmstadt 1968 (Leipzig 1918[1])

Clairmont, F.F.: The Euro Crash, in: Economic and Political Weekly, Vol. 35 (2000), pp. 3644 - 3646

Cobb, C.W./Douglas, P.H.: A Theory of Production, in: American Economic Review, Vol. XVIII (1928), Supplement, pp. 139 – 165

Cohen, B.J.: Enlargement and the International Role of the Euro, in: Review of International Political Economy, Vol. 14 (2007), pp. 746 - 773

Committee on the Working of the monetary system: REPORT, London 1959 (H.M.S.O.; Cmnd. 827)

Culbertson, J.M.: Friedman on the Lag in Effect of Monetary Policy, in: Journal of Political Economy, Vol. 78 (1960), pp. 617 – 621

Duczynski, P.: On the Empirics of Non-Neutrality of Money: Cross-Country Evidence, in: Indian Economic Review, New Series, Vol. 43 (2008), pp. 1 - 15

Duwendag, D.: Akzeptanzprobleme der Europäischen Währungsunion, in: Review of Economics, Vol. 47 (1996), pp. 241 – 263

Eichengreen, B.: The Breakup of the Euro Area, http://eml.berkeley.edu/ (called upon 12.16.2014)

Egle, W.: Das neutrale Geld, Jena 1933

Entschließung des Rates vom 17. Juni 1997 über den Stabilitäts- und Wachstumspakt, ABl. EG Nr. C 236 vom 2. August 1997, S. 1

EU-Kommission: Expertengruppe soll Schuldentilgungsfonds und prüfen, http://ec.europa.eu/ deutschland/press/pr_releases/11527_de.htm (called upon 10.22.2014)

Europäische Kommission: Vorschlag für eine Richtlinie des Europäischen Parlaments und des Rates zum strafrechtlichen Schutz des Euro und anderer Währungen gegen Geldfälschung und zur Ersetzung des Rahmenbeschlusses 2000/383/JI des Rates, COM(2013) 42 final vom 2.5.2013 (2013/0023 (COD))

Europäische Zentralbank: Jahresbericht 2010, Frankfurt am Main 2011

Europäische Zentralbank: Jahresbericht 2011, Frankfurt am Main 2012

Europäische Zentralbank: Jahresbericht 2012, Frankfurt am Main 2013

Europäische Zentralbank: Jahresbericht 2013, Frankfurt am Main 2014

Europäische Zentralbank: Jahresbericht 2014, Frankfurt am Main 2015

Europäische Zentralbank: Monatsbericht Februar 1999, Frankfurt am Main 1999

Eurostat – Tables, Graphs and Maps Interface (TGM) table (http://ec.eurpa.eu/ eurostat/tgm/table.do?tab=table&init=1&language=de&pcode=tec (called upon 06.22.2015)

Fetter, F.W.: Gresham´s Law and the Chilean Peso, in: The Journal of Political Economy, Vol. 41 (1933), pp. 821 – 827

Fisher, I.: The Purchasing Power of Money, New York 1911

Franzius, C./Mayer, F.C./Neyer, J. (Ed.): Grenzen der europäischen Integration, Baden-Baden 2014

Friedman, M.: A Program for money Stability, in: Ketchum, M.D./Kendall, L.T. (Ed.): Readings in Financial Institutions, Boston 1965, pp. 189 - 209

Friedman, M./Meiselman, D.: The relative Stabilitiy of money Velocity and the Investment Multiplier in the United States , 1897 – 1958, in: Commission on Money and Credit: Stabilization Policies, Englewoods Cliffs, N.J. 1963, pp. 165 – 268

Friedman, M./Schwartz, A.: A money History of the United States, 1867 – 1960, Princeton, N.J. 1963

Friedman, M./Schwartz, A.: Die Definition des Geldes: Nettovermögen und Neutralität als Kriterium, in: Brunner, K./Monissen, H.G./Neumann, M.J.M (ed. by): Geldtheorie, Köln 1974, pp. 74 – 90

Friedman, M.: Die optimale Geldmenge und andere Essays, 2nd ed., München 1976 (1970[1])

Friedman, M.: The Lag in Effect of Monetary Policy, in: The Journal Political Economy, Vol. 69 (1961), pp. 447 - 466

Friedman, M.: The Optimum Quantity of Money and Other Essays, London a.o. 1969

Friedman, M.: The Quantity Theory of Money - A Restatement, in: Friedman, M. (Ed.): Studies in the Quantity Theory of Money, Chicago 1956, pp. 3 - 21

Gaskin, M.: Liquidity and money Mechanism, in: Oxford Economic Papers, Vol. 12 (1960), pp. 274 – 293

Gerichtshof der Europäischen Gemeinschaften: Das Europäische Parlament gegen den Rat der Europäischen Gemeinschaft (Klageschrift), Reg.-Nr. 171124, Luxemburg 1983

Gesetz über die Deutsche Bundesbank (BbankG) vom 26.7. 1957 in der Fassung vom 22.10.1992 (BGBl. I S. 1782)

Gesetz zu dem Vertrag vom 2. März 2012 über Stabilität, Koordinierung und Steuerung in der Wirtschafts- und Währungsunion vom 13. September 2012 (BGBl. II, p. 1006)

Gesetz zur Förderung der Stabilität und des Wachstums der Wirtschaft (StabWG) vom 8. Juni 1967 (BGBl. I p. 582), das zuletzt durch Artikel 135 der Verordnung vom 31. Oktober 2006 (BGBl. I p. 2407) geändert worden ist

Gesetz zur Übernahme von Gewährleistungen im Rahmen eines europäischen Stabilisierungsmechanismus (Stabilisierungsmechanismusgesetz – Stab MechG) vom 22. Mai 2010 (BGBl. I p. 627)

Grundgesetz für die Bundesrepublik Deutschland in der im Bundesgesetzblatt Teil III, Gliederungspunkt 100-1, veröffentlichten Fassung, das zuletzt durch Artikel 1 des Gesetzes vom 11. Juli 2012 (BGBL. I p.1478) geändert worden ist

Grundgesetz für die Bundesrepublik Deutschland vom 23. Mai 1949 (BGBl. p. 1; BGBl. III 100-1)

Gurlery, J. G.: The Radcliffe Report and Evidence, in: The American Economic Review, Vol. 50 (1960), pp. 672 – 700

Hauff, V. (Ed.): Unsere gemeinsame Zukunft. Der Brundtland-Bericht, Greven 1987

Hayek, F.A.: Geldtheorie und Konjunkturtheorie, Wien, Leipzig 1929

Hayek, F.v.: Über „neutrales Geld“, in: Zeitschrift für Nationalökonomie, Vol. 4 (1933), pp. 659 - 661

Henkel, H.O.: Rettet unser Geld, 3rd ed., München 2010

Holt, C.C.: Forecasting seasonals and trends by exponentially weighted moving averages, in: International Journal of Forecasting, Vol. 20 (2004), pp. 5 - 10

Holtrop, M.W.: Die Umlaufgeschwindigkeit des Geldes, in: Hayek, F.A. (Ed.): Beiträge zur Geldtheorie, Wien 1933 (reprint Berlin a.o. 2007, pp. 115 – 209)

http:/ec.europa.eu/eurostat/statistics-explained/index.php/National_accounts_GDP (called upon 08.03.2015)

http:/www.sachverständigenrat-wirtschaft.de/zr_deutschland.html (called upon 08.032015)

Hume, D.: Political Discourses, Edinburgh 1752 (reproduction London 2015)

Hunfeld, M.: ESM und Fiskalpakt: Staatsressourcenpolitik für die Europäische Union, in: Meyer, D. (Ed.): Die Zukunft der Währungsunion, Berlin 2012, pp. 135 – 156

Huppert, W.: Neutralität des Geldes, in: Finanzarchiv, Neue Serie, Vol. 4 (1937), pp. 452 – 475

Issing, O.: Einführung in die Geldtheorie, 15th ed., München 2011

Issing, O.: Von der D-Mark zum Euro, Tübingen 1998

Johnson, H.: Neue Entwicklungen in der Geldtheorie: Ein Kommentar, in: Brunner, K./Monissen, H.G./Neumann, M.J.M (Ed.): Geldtheorie, Köln 1974, pp. 26 – 48

Jucker-Fleetwood, E.E.: Der Radcliffe Report, in: Zeitschrift für die gesamte Staatswissenschaft, Vol. 116 (1960), pp. 500 – 517

Kaldor, N.: The Radcliffe Report, in: The Review of Economics and Statistics, Vol. 42 (1960), pp. 14 – 19

Kath, D.: Geld und Kredit, in: Vahlens Kompendium der Wirtschaftstheorie und Wirtschaftspolitik, Vol. 1., 2nd ed., München 1994, pp. 173 – 214

Keuschnigg, C./Weyerstrass, K.: Sollte die EU eine Fiskalunion werden? In: Meyer, D. (Ed.): Die Zukunft der Währungsunion, Münster 2012, pp. 187 - 212

Keynes, J.M.: A treatise of money, London 1930 (German: Keynes, J.M.: Vom Gelde, 3rd ed., Berlin 1983)

Keynes, J.M.: Allgemeine Theorie der Beschäftigung, des Zinses und des Geldes, 11th ed., Berlin 2009

Konvention zum Schutz der Menschenrechte und Grundfreiheiten, vom 4. November 1950 (BGBl. 1952 p. 686)

Koopmans, J.G.: Zum Problem des „Neutralen" Geldes, in: Hayek, F.A. (Ed.): Beiträge zur Geldtheorie, Wien 1933 (reprint Berlin a.o. 2007, pp. 211 – 359)

Krelle, W.: Verteilungstheorie, Wiesbaden 1962

Krystek, U.: Frühwarnsysteme, in: Hutzschenreuter, T./Griess-Nega, T. (Ed.): Krisenmanagement, Wiesbaden 2006, pp. 221 – 244

Lachmann, W. (Ed.).: Die Zukunft des Euro, Münster 2012

Lamine, B.: money and exchange-rate agreements between the European Community and Third Countries, European Commission Directorate-General for Economic and Financial Affairs, Economic Papers, N^0 255, Brussels 2006, pp. 33 – 35 (http://europa.eu. int/comm/economy-finance, called upon 07.09.2015)

Leijonhufvud, A.: On Keynesian Economics and the Economics of Keynes, New York a.o. 1968

Leijonhufvud, A.: Über Keynes und den Keynesianismus, Köln 1973

Luchtmeier, H.: Dollarisierung und Euroisierung, Berlin 2005

Luhmann, N.: Knappheit, Geld und die bürgerliche Gesellschaft, in: Jahrbuch für Sozialwissenschaft, Vol. 23 (1972), pp. 186 - 210

Lutz, F.: Über die Umlaufgeschwindigkeit des Geldes, in: Jahrbücher für Nationalökonomie und Statistik, Vol. 144 (1936), pp. 385 – 409

Lutz, F.: Zur Theorie des Geldmarktes. Zugleich eine Analyse des englischen Geldmarktes bei freier Währung, in: Weltwirtschaftliches Archiv, 42. Vol. (1935), pp. 216 - 247

Mankiv, N.G./Taylor, M.P.: Grundzüge der Volkswirtschaftslehre, 4th ed., Stuttgart 2008

Meyer, D. (Ed.): Die Zukunft der Währungsunion, Münster 2012

Meyer, D.: EURO-Krise. Austritt als Lösung, Berlin 2012

Meyer, D.: Zur juristischen Begründung des „Rettungsschirms": Eine ökonomische Plausibilitätskontrolle, in: Review of Economics, Vol. 61 (2010), pp. 103 - 124

Meyer, F.W.: „Natürliches“ Geld? In: Weltwirtschaftliches Archiv, Vol. 64 (1950), pp. 1 – 11

Meyer, F.W.: „Neutrales“ Geld ist denkbar – aber nicht in einer „natürlichen“ Geldordnung, in: Weltwirtschaftliches Archiv, Vol. 67 (1953), pp. 68 – 73

Moder, M.: Amount Frühwarnsysteme, Wiesbaden 2008

Monissen, H.G.: Die relative Stabilität von Kreislaufgeschwindigkeit des Geldes und Investitionsmultiplikator: Eine Zusammenfassung der Diskussion; in: Brunner, K./Monissen, H.G./Neumann, M.J.M (Ed.): Geldtheorie, Köln 1974, pp. 267 – 289

Moritz, K.-H.: Geldtheorie und Geldpolitik, 3. ed., München 2012

Myrdal, G.: Der Gleichgewichtsbegriff als Instrument der geldtheoretischen Analyse, in: Hayek, F.A. (Ed.): Beiträge zur Geldtheorie, Wien 1933 (reprint Berlin u.a. 2007, pp. 361 – 487)

Negishi, T.: Conditions for Neutral Money, in: The Review of Economic Studdies, Vol. 31 (1964), pp. 147 - 148

Newlyn, W.T.: The Definition of Money: Net Wealth and Neutrality as Criteria: Reply, in: Journal of Money, Credit and Banking, Vol. 4 (1972), pp. 118 – 120

Newlyn, W.T.: Theory of Money, 2nd ed., Oxford 1971 (1962[1])

Paish, F.W.: Was ist Liquidität eigentlich? In: Dürr, E. (Ed.): Geld- und Bankpolitik, 2nd ed., Köln 1971, pp. 283 – 291

Patinkin, D./Steiger, O.: In Search of the „Veil of Money“ and the „Neutrality of Money“: A Note on the Origin of Terms, in: The Scandinavian Journal of Economics, Vol.91 (1989), pp. 131 - 146

Piketty, T.: Das Kapital im 21. Jahrhundert, München 2014

Pullen, J.: The marginal productivity theory of distribution: a critrical history, London 2010

Riese, H.: Theorie der Inflation, Tübingen 1986

Rose, H.B.: Monetary Policy and the Capital Market, 1955-56, in: The Economic Journal, Vol. 67 (1957), pp. 397 – 414

Rugina, A.: Geldtypen und Geldordnungen. Fundamente für eine echte allgemeine Geld- und Wirtschaftstheorie, Stuttgart, Köln 1949

Rugina, A.: Und es kann doch „neutrales“ Geld geben! In: Weltwirtschaftliches Archiv, Vol. 67 (1953), pp. 57 - 68

Sachverständigenrat zur Begutachtung der gesamtwirtschaftlichen Entwicklung: Der Europäische Schuldentilgungspakt – Fragen und Antworten, Arbeitspapier 01/2012, Stand: 25.Januar 2012, http://www.sachverständigenrat-wirtschaft.de (called upon 12.17.2014)

Sauernheimer, K.: Vom Gelde, in: Review of Economics, Vol. 61 (2010), pp. 279 - 299

Schachtschneider, K.A.: Euro-Rettungspolitik – unvernünftig, rechtlos und staatswidrig, in: Lachmann, W. (Ed.): Die Zukunft des Euros, Berlin 2012, pp. 90 – 215

Scharf, F.: Die Finanzkrise als Krise der ökonomischen und rechtlichen Überintegration, in: Franzius, C./Mayer, F.C./Neyer, J. (Ed.): Grenzen der europäischen Integration, Baden-Baden 2014, pp. 51 - 60

Schneider, W.: Früherkennung und Intuition, Wiesbaden 2011

Schuppan, N.: Die Euro-Krise. Ursachen, Verlauf, makroökonomische und europarechtliche Aspekte und Lösungen, München 2014

Selgin, G.: Salvaging Gresham´s Law: The Good, the Bad, and the Illegal, in: Journal of Money, Credit and Banking, Vol. 28 (1996), pp. 637 - 649

Shambaugh, J.C./Reis, R./Rey, H.: The Euro´s Three Crises, in: Brookings Papers on Economic Activity, Spring 2012, pp. 157 – 231

Siebert, H.: Einführung in die Volkswirtschaftslehre, 9th ed., Stuttgart a.o. 1989

Simmel, G.: Philosophie des Geldes, Frankfurt/M. 1969

Sinn, H.-W.: Die Target-Falle. Gefahren für unser Geld und unsere Kinder, München 2012

Six-Pack consisting of:

(1) Verordnung (EU) Nr. 1175/2011 des Europäischen Parlaments und des Rates vom 16. November 2011 zur Änderung der Verordnung (EG) Nr. 1466/97 des Rates über den Ausbau der haushaltspolitischen Überwachung und der Überwachung und Koordinierung der Wirtschaftspolitiken, ABl. EU L 306/12, 23.11.2011

(2) Verordnung (EU) Nr. 1177/2011 des Rates vom 8. November 2011 zur Änderung der Verordnung (EG) Nr. 1467/97 über die Beschleunigung und Klärung des Verfahrens bei einem übermäßigen Defizit, ABl. EU L 306/33, 23.11.2011

(3) Verordnung (EU) Nr. 1173/2011 des Europäischen Parlaments und des Rates vom 16. November 2011 über die wirksame Durchsetzung der haushaltspolitischen Überwachung im Euro-Währungsgebiet, ABl. EU L 306/1, 23.11.2011

(4) Richtlinie 2011/85/EU des Rates vom 8. November 2011 über die Anforderungen an die haushaltspolitischen Rahmen der Mitgliedstaaten, ABl. EU L 306/41, 23.11.2011

(5) Verordnung (EU) Nr. 1176/2011 des Europäischen Parlaments und des Rates vom 16. November 2011 über die Vermeidung und Korrektur makroökonomischer Ungleichgewichte, ABl. EU L 306/25

(6) Verordnung (EU) Nr. 1174/2011 des Europäischen Parlaments und des Rates vom 8. November 2011 über Durchsetzungsmaßnahmen zur Korrektur übermäßiger makroökonomischer Ungleichgewichte im Euro-Währungsgebiet, ABl. EU L 306/8, 23.11.2011

Smith, A.: Der Wohlstand der Nationen, 12th ed., München 2009

Spahn, H.-P.: Geldpolitik. Finanzmärkte, neue Makroökonomie und zinspolitische Strategien, 2nd ed., München 2009

Statistisches Bundesamt (Ed.): Preise. Verbraucherpreisindizes für Deutschland. Lange Reihen ab 1948, Wiesbaden 2015

Statistisches Bundesamt (Ed.): Statistisches Jahrbuch Deutschland und Internationales 2014, Wiesbaden 2014

Statistisches Bundesamt (Ed.): Statistisches Jahrbuch Deutschland und Internationales 2013, Wiesbaden 2013

Statistisches Bundesamt (Ed.): Statistisches Jahrbuch Deutschland und Internationales 2012, Wiesbaden 2012

Statistisches Bundesamt (Ed.): Statistisches Jahrbuch Deutschland und Internationales 2011, Wiesbaden 2011

Statistisches Bundesamt (Ed.): Statistisches Jahrbuch Deutschland und Internationales 2010, Wiesbaden 2010

Statistisches Bundesamt (Ed.): Statistisches Jahrbuch Deutschland und Internationales 2009, Wiesbaden 2009

Statistisches Bundesamt (Ed.): Statistisches Jahrbuch Deutschland und Internationales 2008, Wiesbaden 2008

Statistisches Bundesamt (Ed.): Volkswirtschaftliche Gesamtrechnungen. Bruttoinlandsprodukt ab 1970. Vierteljahres- und Jahresergebnisse. 1. Vierteljahr 2015, Wiesbaden 2015

Streissler, E.W.: Endogenität und Neutralität des Geldes in theoriegeschichtlicher Perspektive, in: Schefold, B. (ed. by): Exogenität und Endogenität. Die Geldmenge in der Geschichte des ökonomischen Denkens und in der modernen Politik, Marburg 2002, pp. 65 - 88

Ströbele, W.: Inflation, 4th ed., München, Wien 1995

Suhr, D.: Geld ohne Mehrwert. Entlastung der Marktwirtschaft von monetären Transaktionskosten, Frankfurt/M. 1983

Suhr, D.: The Capitalistic Cost-Benefit Structure of Money. An Analysis of Money's Structural Nonneutrality and its Effects on the Economy, Berlin, Heidelberg, New York a.o. 1989

Tobin, J.: Ein Allgemeiner Gleichgewichtsansatz zur Geldtheorie, in: Brunner, K./Monissen, H.G./Neumann, M.J.M (Ed.): Geldtheorie, Köln 1974, pp. 219 – 234

Vertrag über die Arbeitsweise der Europäischen Union (konsolidierte Fassung), ABl. EU C 326/47 vom 26.10.2012

Vertrag über die Europäische Union (Maastricht-Vertrag) vom 7. Februar 1992, ABL. EG Nr. C 224 vom 31. August 1992

Vertrag über die Europäische Union (Maastricht-Vertrag) vom 7. Februar 1992 (ABl. EG Nr. C 224 v. 31.8.87. 1992), 6. Protokoll über die Konvergenzkriterien nach Artikel 109j des Vertrages zur Gründung der Europäischen Gemeinschaft

Vertrag über Stabilität, Koordinierung und Steuerung in der Wirtschafts- und Währungsunion zwischen dem Königreich Belgien, der Republik Bulgarien, dem Königreich Dänemark, der Bundesrepublik Deutschland, der Republik Estland, Irland, der Hellenischen Republik, dem Königreich Spanien, der Französischen Republik, der Italienischen Republik, der Republik Zypern, der Republik Lettland, der Republik Litauen, dem Großherzogtum Luxemburg, Ungarn, Malta, dem Königreich der Niederlande, der Republik Österreich, der Republik Polen, der Portugiesischen Republik, Rumänien, der Republik Slowenien, der Slowakischen Republik, der Republik Finnland und dem Königreich Schweden, Titel III, Fiskalpolitischer Pakt vom 2. März 2012 (BGBl. II, S. 1008)

Vertrag zur Errichtung des Europäischen Stabilitätsmechanismus zwischen dem Königreich Belgien, der Bundesrepublik Deutschland, der Republik Estland, Irland, der Hellenischen Republik, dem Königreich Spanien, der Französischen Republik, der Italienischen Republik, der Republik Zypern, dem Großherzogtum Luxemburg, Malta, dem Königreich der Niederlande, der Republik Österreich, der Portugiesischen Republik, der Republik Slowenien, der Slowakischen Republik und der Republik Finnland vom 2. Februar 2012 (BGBl. II, S. 981, 983)

Vertrag zur Gründung der Europäischen Wirtschaftsgemeinschaft vom 25. März 1957 (BGBL. II S. 766)

Vertrag zur Gründung der Europäischen Wirtschaftsgemeinschaft vom 25. März 1957 (BGBL. II S. 766), in der Fassung des Vertrages über die Europäische Union vom 7. Februar 1992, ABL. EG Nr. C 224 vom 31. August 1992, S. 6

Vertrag zur Gründung der Europäischen Gemeinschaft, Protokoll (Nr. 4), Über die Satzung des Europäischen Systems der Zentralbanken und der Europäischen Zentralbank, ABl. EU, C 83/230 vom 30.3.2010

Wagner, H.-J.: Stabiles oder neutrales Geld: Eine ordnungspolitische Diskussion, in: Neuere Entwicklungen in der Geldtheorie und Geldpolitik, ed. by Bofinger, P./Ketterer, K.-H., Tübingen 1996, pp. 71 – 90

Walras, L.: Elements d´économie politique pure ou théorie de la richesse sociale, Lausanne, Paris, Bale (Basel) 1874

Wicksell, K.: Geldzins und Güterpreis, München 2006 (Original Jena 1898)

Wicksell, K.: Interest and Prices, London 1936

Willgerodt, H.: Politische Union als Voraussetzung einer Währungsunion? In: Neuere Entwicklungen in der Geldtheorie und Geldpolitik, ed. by Bofinger, P./Ketterer, K.-H., Tübingen 1996, pp. 137 - 163

Willms, M.: Das Gleichgewichtsproblem in der klassischen und neoklassischen Geldtheorie, in: Jahrbuch für Sozialwissenschaft, Vol. 17 (1966), pp. 166 - 197

Willms, M.: Grundprobleme der europäischen Währungsintegration, in: Weltwirtschaftliches Archiv, Vol. 108 (1972), pp. 43 - 50

Willms, M.: Zahlungsbilanz, Wechselkurs und Währungssysteme, in: Vahlens Kompendium der Wirtschaftstheorie und Wirtschaftspolitik, Vol. 1, 2th ed., München 1984, pp. 215 – 253

Witte, H.: Die Bedeutung der Kreditgenossenschaften für die regionale Entwicklung, in: Research & Statistic, Vol. 3 (1984), pp. 101 - 119

Witte, H.: Die nachhaltige Marktwirtschaft. Wohlstand ohne „self-made" Krisen? Berlin 2013 (Englisch: Sustainable Market Ecomony. Welfare without self-made crises? Zürich 2015)

Witte, H.: Die Szczecin-Gleichung, in: Witte, H.: The Szczecin School of „simple" Economics, Szczecin 2010, pp. 35 - 44

Witte, H.: Eine Untersuchung der kreditwirtschaftlichen Versorgung der Regionen in Nordrhein-Westfalen, Opladen 1981

Witte, H.: The money Production Function as a Basis of Sustainability, in: edited by Witte, H. a.o.: Sustainable Logistics, Bahia Blanca 2012, pp. 13 – 23

Wittmann, W.: Von der Finanzkrise zur Schuldenkrise, in: Review of Economics, Vol. 62 (2011), pp. 40 - 55

Woll, A.: Quantitätstheorie, in: Handwörterbuch der Wirtschaftswissenschaft (HdWW), 6. Vol., Stuttgart a.o. 1981, pp. 392 – 399

Subject Index